IMAGES
of America

WASHINGTON
GEORGIA

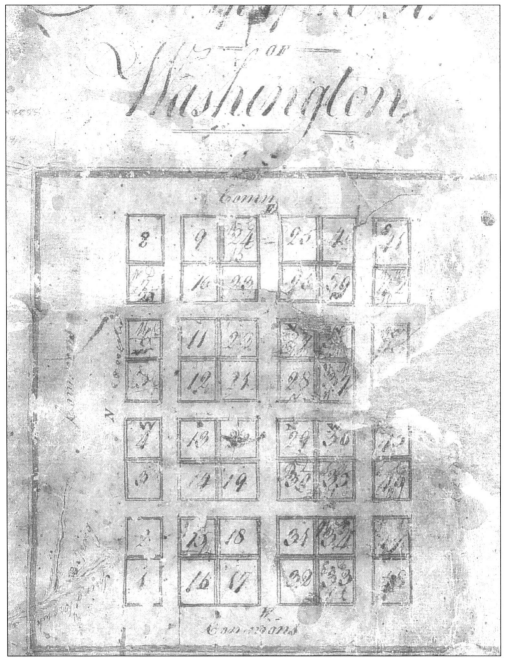

Washington was chartered in 1780 and laid out in a grid pattern, surrounded by a town commons. This map probably dates from 1783, when the town lots were being sold and the earliest settlers were establishing this as their home. (Courtesy Mary Willis Library.)

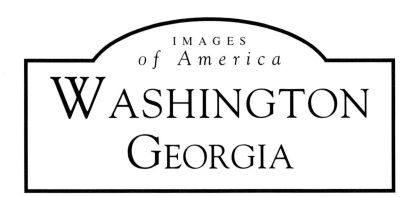

Robert M. Willingham Jr.

Copyright © 2000 by Robert M. Willingham Jr.
ISBN 978-0-7385-0571-8

Published by Arcadia Publishing
Charleston, South Carolina

Printed in the United States of America

Library of Congress Catalog Card Number: 00-103696

For all general information contact Arcadia Publishing at:
Telephone 843-853-2070
Fax 843-853-0044
E-mail sales@arcadiapublishing.com
For customer service and orders:
Toll-Free 1-888-313-2665

Visit us on the Internet at www.arcadiapublishing.com

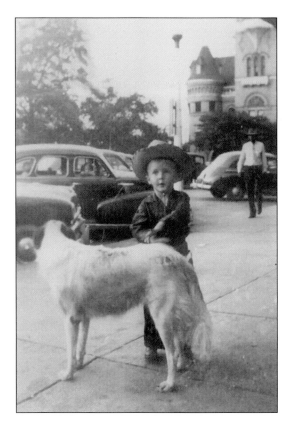

The author and his trusty companion "Happy" share a special time on the Washington town square in 1949.

CONTENTS

Acknowledgments — 6

Introduction — 7

1. An Eventful History — 9

2. Centered on a Square — 29

3. Economic Ventures — 39

4. Home and Hearth — 59

5. Educating the People — 75

6. Strong in Spirit — 91

7. Leisure and Society — 107

ACKNOWLEDGMENTS

A project such as this is always a collaborative effort. The cooperation of the Washington-Wilkes community has been truly heartwarming to me; it has also made this a better and more representative volume. My particular thanks go to Celeste Stover and her amazingly able staff at the Mary Willis Library for sharing the jewels of their outstanding collection. Olive Wills, curator of the Washington Historical Museum, Washington's Mayor and City Council, and Sandy White, Main Street Director, arranged, granted permission, and coordinated the copying of wonderful hitherto unpublished images from the museum's holdings. Mrs. Jo R. Randall has graciously allowed the use of certain photographs from her fine work, *Washington After 200 Years*. Heather Martin and the helpful staff at Fievet Pharmacy have made copy services available with incredible efficiency. Mercer Harris and Glenn Weber, photographers par excellence in their own right, have copied images, and Mercer has been most generous in sharing from his own treasure trove of local photographs. Images from the estates of the late Dr. J.T. Bryson and the late Mrs. Mary Ficklen Barnett have been made available and are now shared with the public. Mrs. Shari Bryson, C. Carol Cartledge, Lee Connell, Paula Drexler, Mrs. Mary Johnson Duggan, Don Fucich, Henry Harris Jr., Mrs. Elizabeth M. Ivey, Willis Lindsey, C.H. Randall Jr., Dr. Kittrell Rushing, Betty Slaton, Dawn Walker, Patricia D. Wilder, my uncle, C.M. Willingham, and my mother, Mrs. Helen A. Willingham, have all provided fascinating images for this volume and have been sources of inspiration and encouragement.

INTRODUCTION

On June 11, 1773, a treaty between James Wright (Georgia's royal governor) and chiefs of the Creek and Cherokee Nations ceded a strategic parcel of land north and west of Augusta to the colony of Georgia. This land, rich with lush Piedmont forests and grazing land prime for development, quickly began to fill with settlers from Virginia and the Carolinas, and as far distant as Pennsylvania and the isles of the West Indies. The area would become Wilkes County in 1777, the first county designated in the first constitution for a new and independent Georgia.

Soon after the initial wave of settlement came the Americans' valiant struggle for independence. At the conclusion of these hostilities, pioneers would once again pour into the territory. In upcountry Georgia the Revolutionary War literally pitted brother against brother as this newest of British colonies still held close ties to the Motherland. On Valentine's Day, 1779, Wilkes Countians and other patriots attacked and soundly defeated a Tory force on Kettle Creek in the lower part of the county. Local citizens like Elijah Clarke, Austin Dabney, and Nancy Hart were memorable examples of bravery for their fellow settlers.

Washington received its charter on January 23, 1780, becoming the first town in the United States to be chartered in the name of the commander-in-chief of American forces. By 1783, the town had been laid out with a public square, town common, and plans for a "Latin and grammar school." However, the area was still "rough-and-tumble," as the frontier lifestyle was not one in which gentility could prosper. Sarah Hillhouse, a proper New Englander removed to this Georgia frontier village, remarked in the 1780s that many of Washington's inhabitants were "the most profane and blasphemous sort." Fortunately, with community, education, and stability came civilization and refinement, and by the early 1800s, Washington-Wilkes was being compared to Charleston for charm and culture.

An economic explosion occurred soon after Eli Whitney's perfection of the cotton gin. In 1810, the Bolton Factory was begun near Washington as the first cotton mill established in the South. The local economy, which had been tobacco-based, almost overnight geared itself to cotton production. The plantation era meant unparalleled prosperity for some, and it was during this period that many local homes were embellished with colonnades of impressive proportions.

Politically, too, antebellum Wilkes was a force far greater than its number of citizens would indicate. Ten of Georgia's governors prior to 1860 had their roots in the soil of Old Wilkes. Because of the early-19th-century feud between political giants John Clark and William H. Crawford in Washington Tavern and Courthouse, two-party politics in Georgia was born. With Robert Toombs leading the way, Washington-Wilkes was a hotbed of secession sentiment and, although not all citizens were rabid rebels, locals were vigorously supportive of the Confederacy.

Four Wilkes units marched boldly to battle, but many of the soldiers did not return. The Irvin Guard became an artillery company in Cutts Battalion at Gettysburg, where it performed heroically. Following the euphoria of the first days of the conflict, a gradual battle-weariness settled into soldier and homefolk alike. There were rumors of war locally, but Sherman never came.

Following the fall of Richmond, the little town of Washington became the central focus for the fleeing government of the Confederate States. In May of 1865, President Jefferson Davis, his military advisors, and remaining cabinet officers met together in the Old Bank Building for the last official meeting of the Confederacy. Davis signed his final papers, military payrolls were distributed, and a decision was made to disperse. The central government of the Confederate States of America had now disbanded and Washington was witness to the somber event.

Monies from both the Confederate treasury and Virginia banks were stored in Washington vaults. These assets were seized only hours after Davis and his entourage fled as Federal troops poured into town. While the "Confederate Gold" was being transported to the North at the end of May, the Federal wagon train was attacked by Confederate faithful a few miles outside Washington and some of the gold vanished, never to be recovered.

For several years following the war, Wilkes County experienced occupation by Federal military forces and was subject to martial law. Reconstruction brought forth political activism by African-American citizens for the first time, and saw the emergence of separate churches and the initial efforts toward developing black educational institutions.

With the old order passed away, there was an almost immediate influx of new settlers with entrepreneurial ambitions. The railroad grew in importance, and it took little time for new businesses and buildings to spring forth. Cotton still ruled, though now tenancy had replaced slavery as the method for employing workers in the fields. An annual agricultural fair was begun that not only promoted local farming interests but also made available the latest in agricultural advancements.

As a new century dawned so did economic prosperity for Wilkes County. A building boom was on. Four banks were successfully operating in Washington. Automobiles gradually replaced the railroad as the major method of transportation, and a solid system of roads was coming about. Semi-professional baseball was the popular diversion of the day. World Wars united the whole community to work for the greater good.

The demolition of the historic Old Bank Building in 1904 to make way for a new courthouse sparked the development of one of the nation's first organizations to actively promote the importance of historic preservation. Washington-Wilkes is thus blessed that so many significant structures from its history still remain.

Community exuberance was shaken to its foundation by the destruction wrought by the boll weevil. The devastation spelled the end to an economy dependent for over a century on cotton; coupled with the Great Depression, it forced a thorough reassessment of the direction the local economy would take. Farmers were forced to diversify. Industries, too, began to arrive. First came textiles, then wood products, plastics, fiberglass, dyes, and others utilizing the latest in high technology.

Today Washington-Wilkes is a modern community that cherishes its heritage. There are good schools, spirit-filled churches, a diversified economy, recreational opportunities, and people who work together and truly care about one another. Each day a new page of this area's storied history is being written, with reverence and sensitivity for that which is past and anticipation for that which is to come.

One

AN EVENTFUL HISTORY

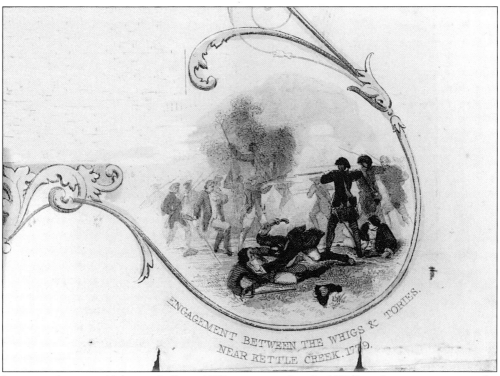

Just past dawn on Valentine's Day, 1779, a rag-tag band of Wilkes County patriots under Colonels Elijah Clarke and John Dooly, along with South Carolina soldiers under Andrew Pickens, attacked an unsuspecting group of Tories led by Colonel Boyd of North Carolina near Kettle Creek in south Wilkes County. Surprised by the onslaught, the Tories retreated in disarray. This American victory proved highly significant for the fledgling state of Georgia as it thwarted the British attempt to control the entire region. Wilkes County accurately earned its Revolutionary War sobriquet "The Hornet's Nest."

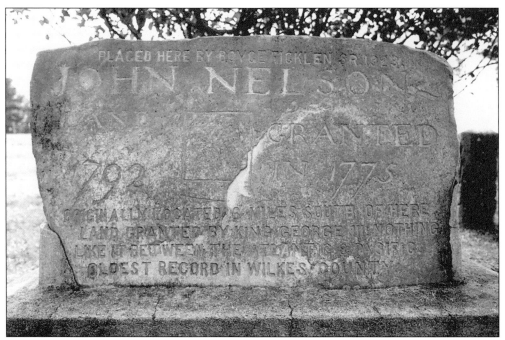

One of the earliest relics of Wilkes County's settlement is the so-called "John Nelson Rock." This was a stone carved and placed on land granted to Nelson in 1775 and incised with his name and the date. The stone was moved to Washington in 1923 by Boyce Ficklen Sr., and is now situated in Fort Washington Park.

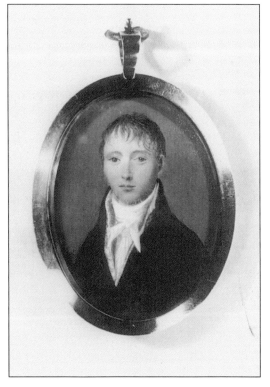

Andrew Green Simpson Semmes (1781–1833) moved to Washington in 1800 as a young man seeking his "fortune" in the bustling new town. He became a leading planter and merchant, as well as ruling elder of the Presbyterian Church. Among his children was Albert Gallatin Semmes, an accomplished architect who designed several area homes. (Courtesy Mary Willis Library.)

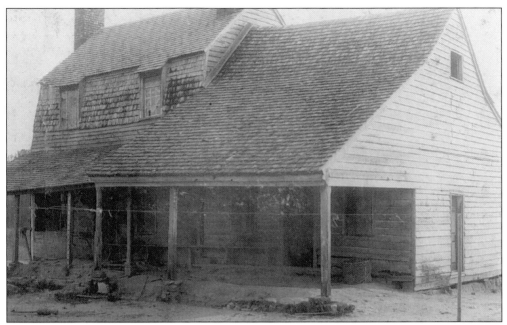

The Talbot family came to Wilkes County in the 1780s from Maryland and quickly established themselves as major landowners. The gambrel-roofed section of this house was constructed about 1783 for John Talbot on a plantation several miles east of Washington on the old Augusta Post Road. This was the childhood residence of Georgia governor Matthew Talbot. The structure was razed shortly after this 1880s photograph was taken. (Courtesy Mary Willis Library.)

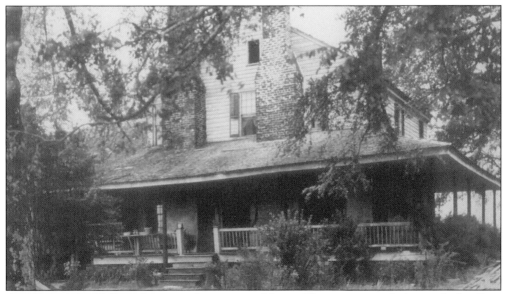

Another of the Talbot plantation houses was Mount Pleasant, a regal plainstyle dwelling erected about 1790 by Thomas Talbot. It was near this home that Eli Whitney experimented with his cotton gin while serving as a tutor to the Talbot children. The Burdett family had assumed the plantation when this c. 1900 image was commissioned. (Courtesy Washington Historical Museum.)

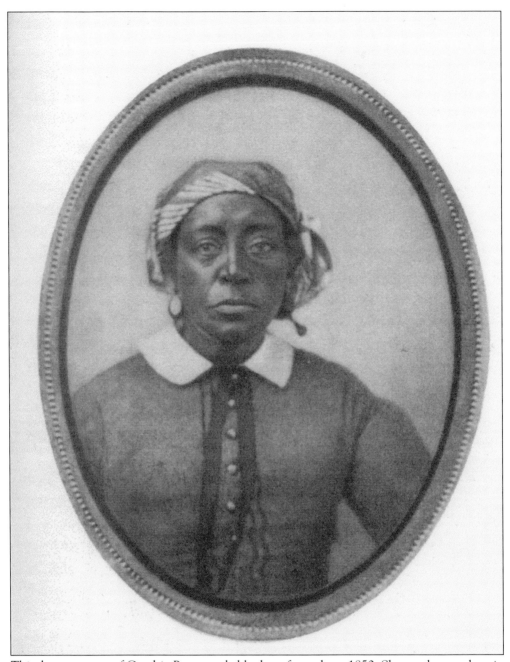

This daguerreotype of Cynthia Peters probably dates from about 1850. She was born a slave in the household of Felix Gilbert and became a beloved confidante of the Alexander family. One of the children she helped to raise, Mary Clifford Alexander Hull, described her as having "an eagle eye for deviations from the path of rectitude and virtue."

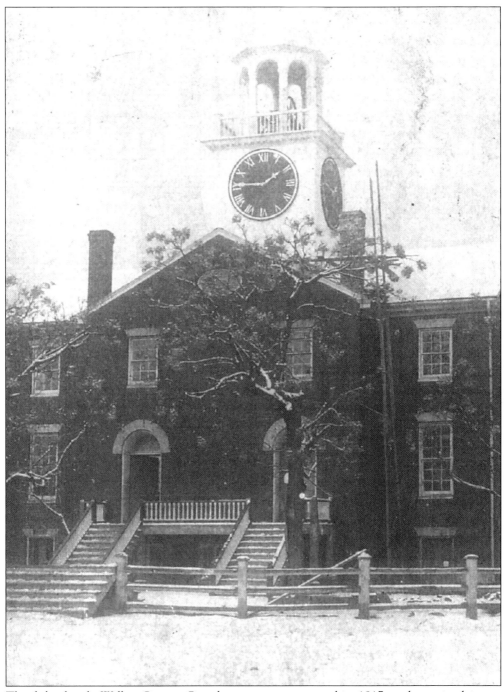

The federal-style Wilkes County Courthouse was constructed in 1817, and remained in use until the present courthouse was completed in 1904. When John Quincy Adams was elected in the intense 1824 presidential campaign, one local partisan wished to celebrate the victory by ringing the courthouse bell. Prevented by supporters of unsuccessful candidate Andrew Jackson, the Adams advocate climbed the outside wall of the tower to strike the bell with a hammer. (Courtesy Mary Willis Library.)

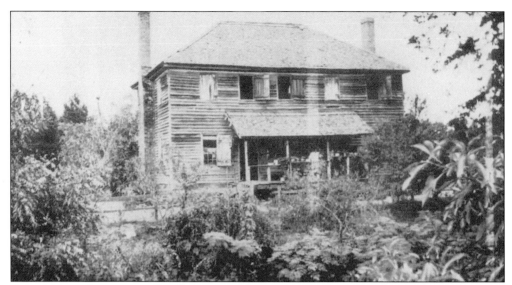

Situated on what is now South Smyrna Church Road east of Washington, the home of Abraham Simons served as both a residence and a popular inn. Simons was a Revolutionary War veteran, merchant, and state legislator (1805–1806) married to Nancy Mills. The house no longer stands but Simons is buried nearby, reputedly standing up with a musket in his hand so he could fight off the Devil. His widow later married Rev. Jesse Mercer.

One of the earliest volumes of Washington's town ordinances is this one printed by Philip C. Guieu in 1822. Guieu was editor and publisher of the local newspaper and proprietor of the only press in town. The mayor (then called president) of Washington at that time was Gilbert Hay. (Courtesy Mary Willis Library.)

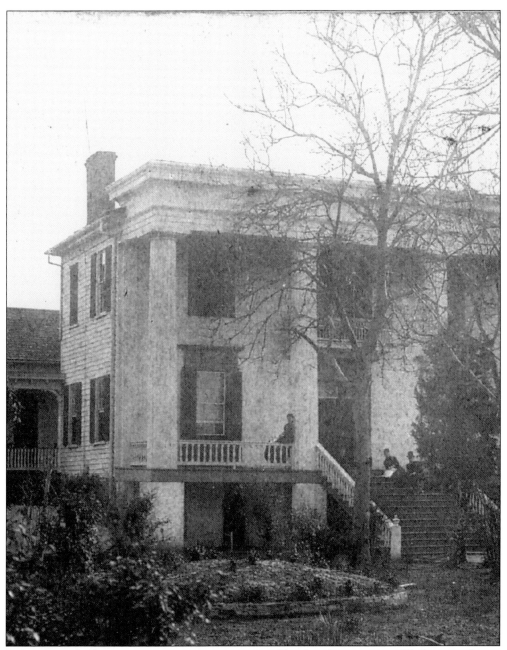

Robert Toombs' home is now a state historic site and landmark structure in Washington. It was built by Joel Abbott, a doctor and congressman, and later enlarged by Judge William Harris. Toombs brought the home to its present standing, adding the distinctive portico, and had a law office located in the basement of the center section of the house. The house was filled with the vibrancy of history. From the balcony, Toombs, on several occasions, would regale his admiring audiences with enthusiastic exhortations rallying Wilkes Countians to his causes. Federal troops occupied the home in the summer of 1865, and were literally knocking on the front door as Toombs fled out the back avoiding capture. For a brief while the house was used to garrison troops and as a school for newly freed African-American children.

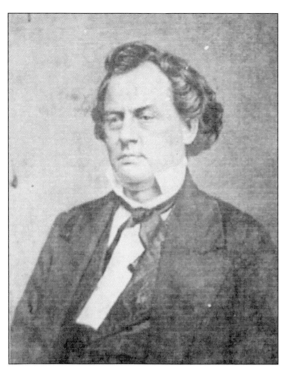

Of all Washingtonians, no citizen held so great a reputation in the 19th century as Robert Toombs (1810–1885). He had a distinguished antebellum career as a planter, lawyer, U.S. representative, and U.S. senator. Strongly considered for the presidency of the Confederacy, he was selected to serve as its secretary of state. He later resigned to assume a field commission in the Confederate Army as general. At the close of the war, Toombs daringly escaped from Federal troops and spent almost two years in exile in Cuba and Europe. Never accepting the oath of allegiance to the United States, he considered himself Georgia's "unreconstructed rebel." In 1877, Toombs led the agrarian interests in constructing a new Georgia state constitution.

Edward Porter Alexander was a recent graduate of West Point when shots were fired at Fort Sumter. He resigned his United States commission and joined the Confederate service. By the Battle of Gettysburg he was serving as General Longstreet's chief of artillery. His innovative and perceptive ideas helped to modernize the signal service as well as the artillery. Alexander rose to the rank of brigadier general. After the War between the States, he became a professor of engineering, railroad president, rice planter, and author.

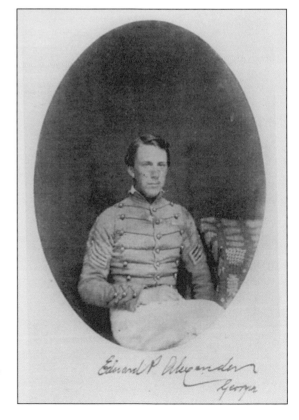

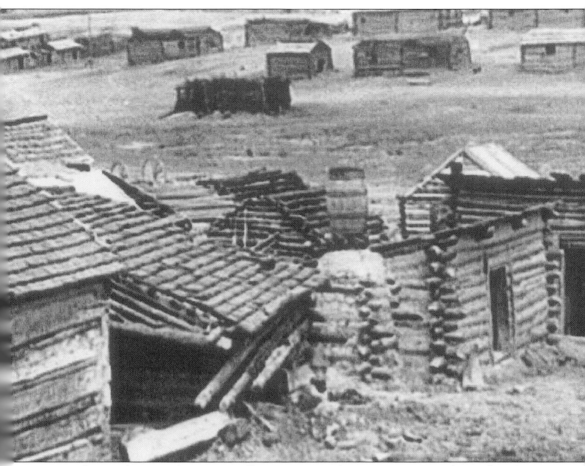

During the War between the States, Wilkes County sent four major units into the conflict. One of these, the Irvin Guard, had a preponderance of men from the town of Washington. Led by Capt. John T. Wingfield, the troops were made into an artillery brigade and valiantly fought at Gettysburg as a part of Cutts' Battalion. In the winter of 1861–62, the Irvin Guard settled into quarters at Centreville, VA, until spring fighting began. Each "mess" was responsible for constructing and maintaining its own cabin during the cold, wet season. James Hillhouse Alexander, a private in the company, wrote the following to his father on December 27, 1861: "The 'Irvin Artillery' moved out to new ground last week and at once began work on their winter huts . . . Thirteen nice log cabins, 10 for men and 3 for officers are far progressed, and were today allotted out, each to be completed by its occupants. And now in four days they will be in them and living comfortably. 14 by 18 is the size and eight men in each, which will give room enough for all who have been living in a tent of 10 by 10." The esteemed photographer George Barnard captured the camp on film in March 1862. (Courtesy Library of Congress.)

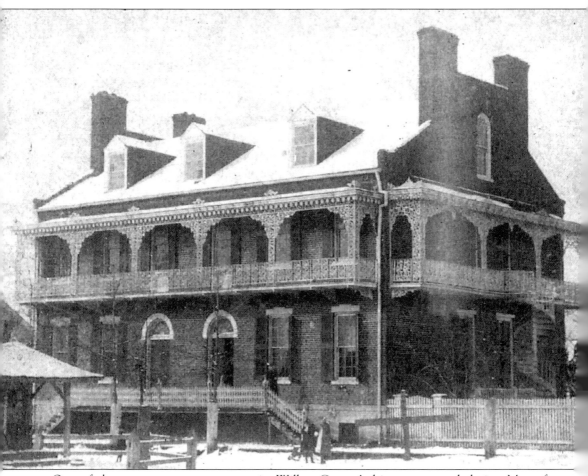

One of the most momentous events in Wilkes County's history occurred during May of 1865. General Lee had surrendered his Confederates on April 9 at Appomattox, VA, and General Johnston's troops followed suit on April 26 at Greensboro, NC. Richmond, the Confederate capital, had fallen and President Jefferson Davis, his family, and closest associates fled southward seeking refuge from the onrushing Federals. According to Treasurer Micajah Clark, Washington, GA, was "where the bitter end was reached—the welcome, though fearful, was filled with warmth and tenderness." It was at the Bank of the State of Georgia building that Davis spent the night of May 4 and there he conferred with his remaining cabinet officers and military advisors for the last time, signing the final documents of the Confederate government.

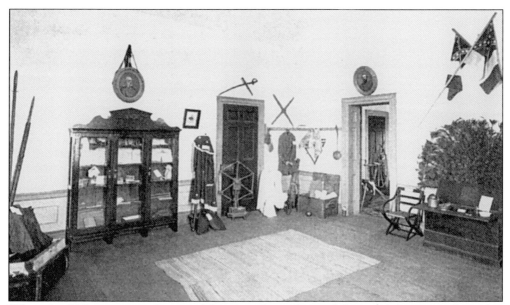

When the Wilkes County chapter of the United Daughters of the Confederacy was formed in 1895, they set about establishing a museum in the room where President Davis last met with his cabinet in the Old Bank Building. Among the items preserved was Davis's own camp chest. Most of these relics are now housed in the Washington Historical Museum.

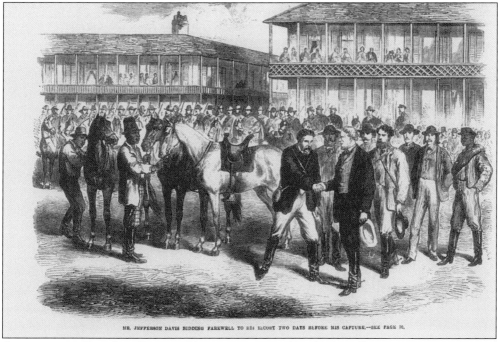

Accompanying President Davis and his entourage was Frank Vizetelly, an artist commissioned by the *London Illustrated News* and *Harpers* Magazine to document pictorially the last days of the Confederacy. Here, Davis shakes the hand of Rev. Henry Allen Tupper, local Baptist minister, as they stand in the Washington town square. He bids adieu to his guard and the townspeople of Washington, who greeted him with hospitality and sympathy.

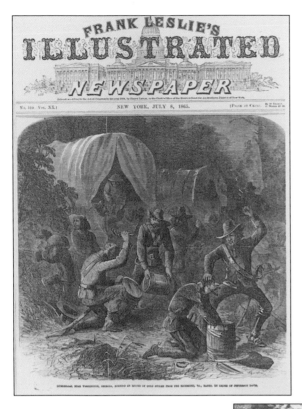

One of the most exciting episodes in local history was the raid and robbery of the wagon train hauling Confederate gold and bank monies back northward under Federal guard. At Chennault Plantation, some 15 miles northeast of Washington, Confederate stragglers ransacked the wagons on the evening of May 24, 1865, in an attempt to "repatriate" the fortune from the Union soldiers. It made national news as the cover of *Leslie's* popular magazine attests. Some of the gold was never recovered, and the legend persists to the present day.

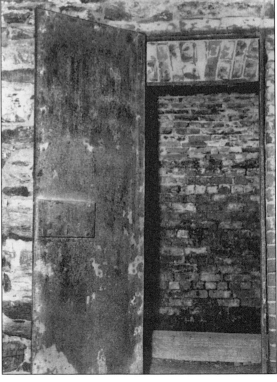

This vault in the basement of the stagecoach inn at the south end of the Square (now Scarborough's) stored the gold and silver bars and coinage from the Virginia banks prior to the trek northward, which ended in disaster at Chennault.

W. Alexander Hardy served faithfully as a private in the Irvin Guard during the War between the States. When the local chapter of the United Confederate Veterans Association was formed, he became one of its first members. In this turn-of-the-20th-century view he is shown proudly wearing his reunion badges.

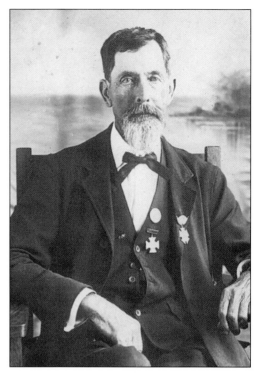

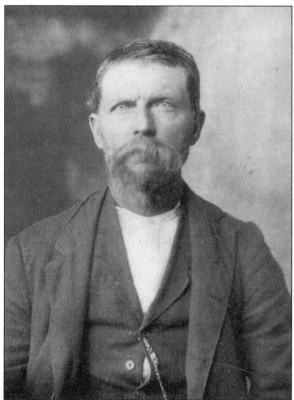

Patrick Hugh Mansfield was born in 1846 in South Carolina into an Irish-Catholic family that soon after moved to Wilkes County. As a 16 year old he enlisted as a private in Company A of the First Georgia Troops, and served briefly at the defenses around Atlanta. He died in 1918 and is buried at St. Patrick's Catholic Cemetery in Washington. (Courtesy Mrs. John H Ivey.)

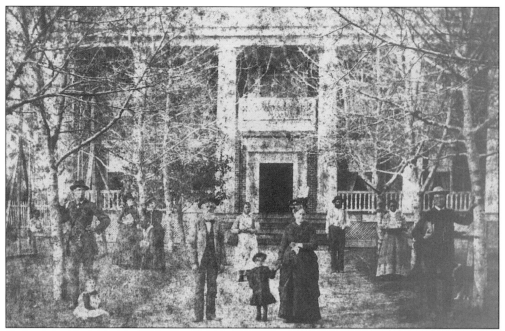

One of the first local efforts toward rebuilding after the war came in 1869 when Aristides Callaway began the erection of this two-story brick house on his plantation, some 4 miles west of Washington on the road to Athens. The bricks were made locally, and with its classic Greek Revival portico, the home would become one of the final examples of what was considered "planter" architecture. The Callaway clan and household servants are shown in this photograph from the last quarter of the 19th century. (Courtesy estate of Dr. J.T. Bryson.)

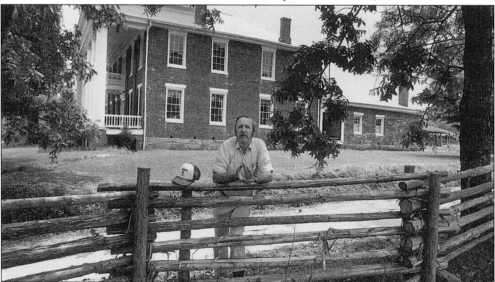

The preservation of history is held in high regard in Washington-Wilkes. This community believes in sharing its heritage with future generations. A leader in Washington's preservation movement was Dr. J.T. Bryson, who spearheaded and shepherded the Callaway Restoration Site for almost three decades. His knowledge and enthusiasm remind those who have come after him of how important such a task truly is. (Courtesy Mercer Harris.)

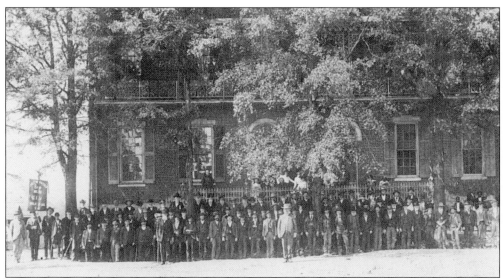

By the 1890s, the United Confederate Veterans were well organized and enthusiastic. Tradition and remembrance played a strong role in postbellum Wilkes County. The Old Bank Building, then referred to as the Heard House, was a popular spot for group photographs. (Courtesy Mary Willis Library.)

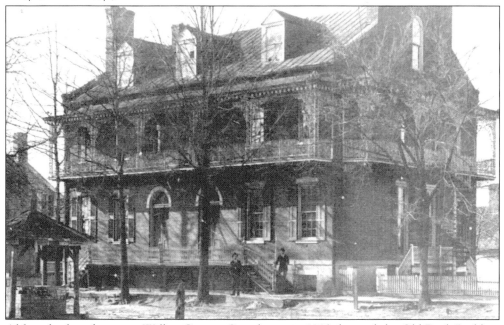

Although plans for a new Wilkes County Courthouse in 1903 doomed the Old Bank Building to destruction, that was not the initial desire of most locals. The *Washington Gazette* in January 1900 commented on a county idea to retain the old structure for offices and erect a new courthouse on an adjacent lot: "In this way the old historic building in which the last meeting of the Confederate Cabinet was held, will be preserved intact, and it will be the better for being occupied and used daily. Old Independence Hall in Philadelphia, where the first American congress met, is itself occupied and used for the sake of better preserving it." (Courtesy Mary Willis Library.)

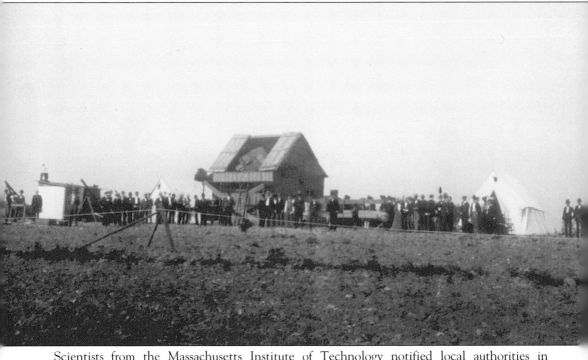

Scientists from the Massachusetts Institute of Technology notified local authorities in January 1900 that a sizable team of researchers would be visiting Washington in late May to observe the total solar eclipse. Their analysis had determined that Washington was one of the prime spots on the planet from which to view this phenomenon. The observation post was a cotton field at the southern end of town, which provided unobstructed views to allow the scientific equipment maximum effectiveness. Astronomers from M.I.T. as well as Harvard, Creighton, Saint Louis, Xavier, Blue Hill, and Flagstaff made Washington headquarters. The new local hotels, the Johnson and the Fitzpatrick, did a booming business. In addition to a main building housing the telescope, nicknamed "Jumbo," the scientists erected tents and other temporary structures over the property to gather a variety of measurements. Several schoolgirls of the community were called into duty to provide sketches of the eclipse as it reached its peak. Washington's hospitality was so gracious that one of the M.I.T. photographers remarked upon leaving, "What a pity it is that eclipses never strike the same place twice in a fellow's lifetime." (Courtesy Washington Historical Museum.)

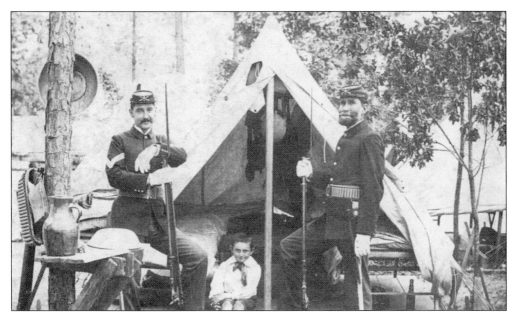

In July 1901, Washington hosted the encampment for the Third Georgia Regiment of state militia. The site selected was Effie Pope Park, west of downtown. Almost 400 soldiers were in residence from as far away as Augusta and Conyers at the facility dubbed Camp Dyson, named in honor of Washington mayor J.R. Dyson. A young boy views with fascination the tent and uniforms of these members of the Irvin Guards. Maj. Anson King and Capt. Harry Smith were leaders of the local unit. (Courtesy C.H. Randall Jr.)

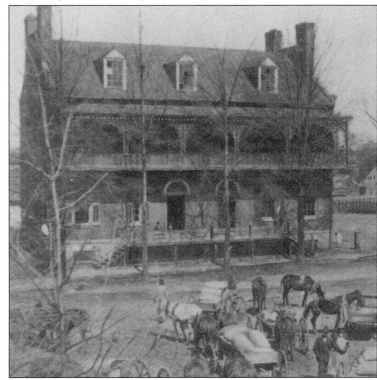

Mules and horses graze before the Old Bank Building shortly before construction began on the new courthouse just to its rear. In the distance at the right are houses on Alexander Avenue, two blocks to the east.

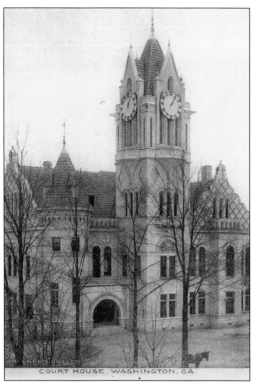

Formal notice for a new courthouse was issued by the commissioners on May 1, 1903. Architect Frank Milburn was awarded the contract, with Savannah Contracting Company and J.E. Burgess superintending the construction. By June 1904, the finishing touches were being placed on the massive Flemish-design structure. (Courtesy Mary Willis Library.)

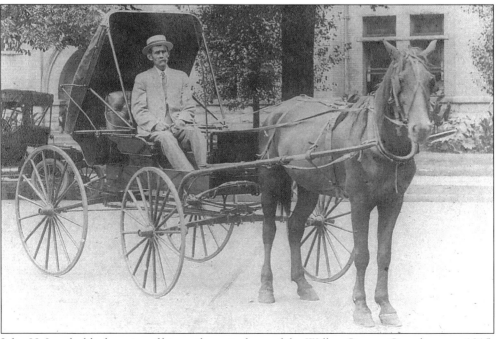

John H. Ivey holds the reins of his mail cart in front of the Wilkes County Courthouse c. 1915. Ivey was one of the first rural mail carriers in the area from the early days of rural free delivery. He even invented a swing-away mail box, particularly useful beside country roads. (Courtesy Mrs. John H. Ivey.)

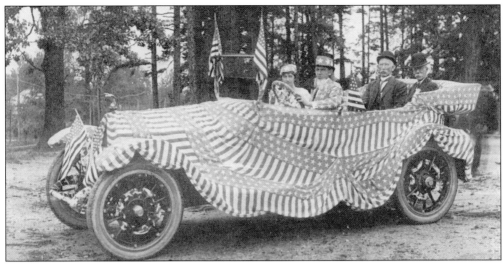

Possibly celebrating the armistice, Washingtonians patriotically bedecked a touring car to honor America. The occupants of the vehicle, from left to right, are Rosa Hill Strickland, Garnett A. Green, J. Luke Burdett, and Edward A. Barnett. (Courtesy estate of Mrs. Mary F. Barnett.)

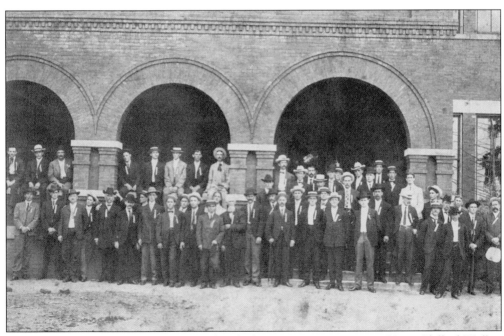

Political campaigns always drew a crowd and often passionate responses. Here, Clifford Walker of Winder brought his gubernatorial effort to rally at Washington High School in 1923.

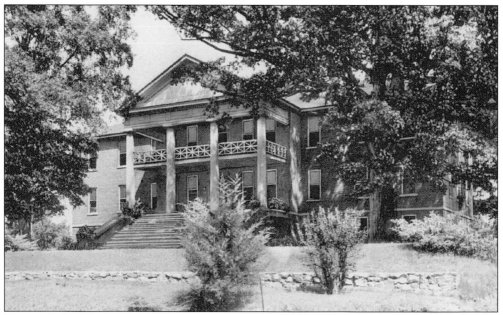

Determined community effort insured that 15 years of planning and work toward a hospital for Washington would not be in vain. By 1924, Dr. C.E. Wills was named general manager of the new facility. His words resound clearly today: "A good hospital is the life of a community. And it is built not for a day, but to last as long as the town in which it is situated." (Courtesy Mary Willis Library.)

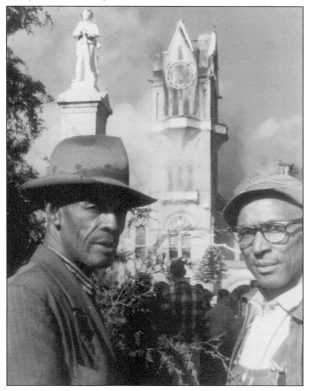

Just before Christmas 1958, Washington looked in horror as fire ravaged the Wilkes County Courthouse. Smoke and flames quickly spread throughout the historic structure, and tongues of fire lapped through the roof and tower. By the time the blaze was brought under control, the upper stories and tower lay in ruins, but the building and its records had been saved. Carey Ware (at right) and an unidentified gentleman look on as fire bursts forth from the clock tower. (Courtesy Mercer Harris.)

Two
Centered on a Square

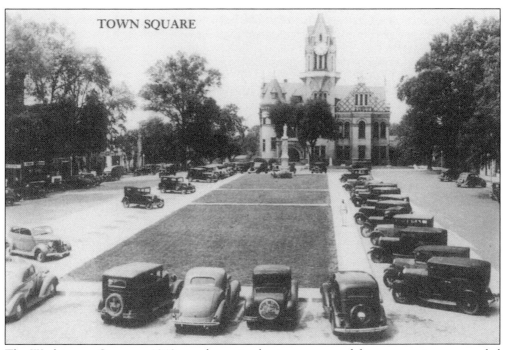

The Washington Square c. 1940 was the active business center of the community, surrounded by stores providing virtually all the mercantile needs for the area. The bustling businesses and sidewalks contrast with the serene grassy sward at the square's center. Almost from the town's inception, the square has been a meeting place, economic hub, and center of activity.

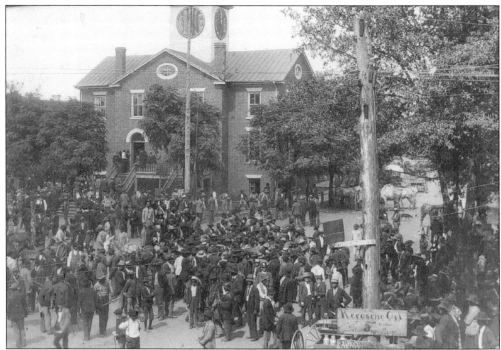

The old courthouse on the square witnessed a throng of people on a spring day in 1895 when Washington's resident photographers, Hodgson and Goodman, took this view. Only a few months later the west square would be devastated by the Great Fire of 1895. Whether this was a political rally or court was in full session is not known, but it was clearly a social occasion. (Courtesy Mary Willis Library.)

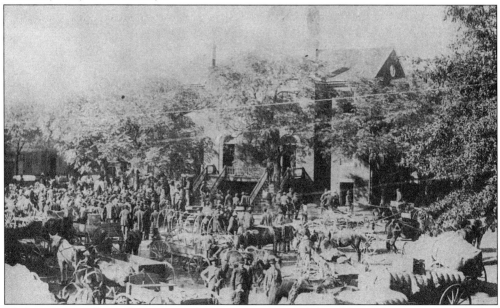

With wagons and people jamming the square in front of the old courthouse, it appears that "Sale Day" was well underway around the turn of the 20th century. (Courtesy estate of Mrs. Mary F. Barnett.)

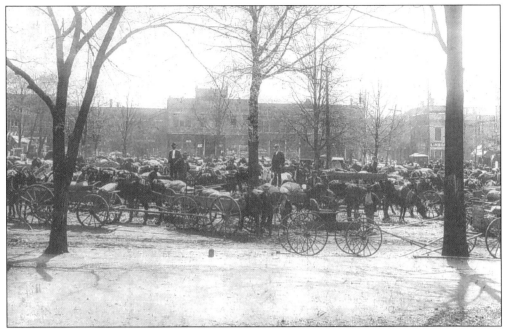

Looking southward on the square, wagons are massed for Sale Day. After an 1898 fire, new buildings were constructed by Anson King and for Mrs. W.W. Simpson by African-American contractor Edward Bonner. These are visible in the center background. To their right is the store of J.T. Lindsey. (Courtesy Lee Connell and Willis Lindsey.)

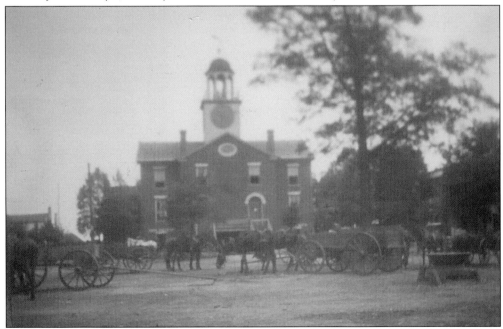

In the spring of 1900, the square was a convenient place for farmers to deposit their wagons and mules while they visited the local merchants to buy, sell, and barter. In the right foreground is a watering trough for the various beasts of burden. The 1817 courthouse stands sentinel at the center background. (Courtesy Washington Historical Museum.)

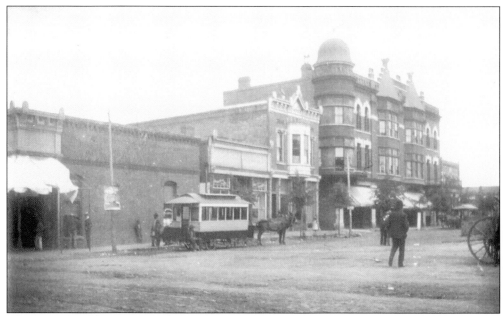

The west side of the square displays a variety of businesses in the new brick buildings, all erected between late 1895 and May 1900, when this photograph was taken. Both the incoming and outgoing trolleys of the street railroad are visible in front of the corner drug store and further back at the Fitzpatrick Hotel. (Courtesy Washington Historical Museum.)

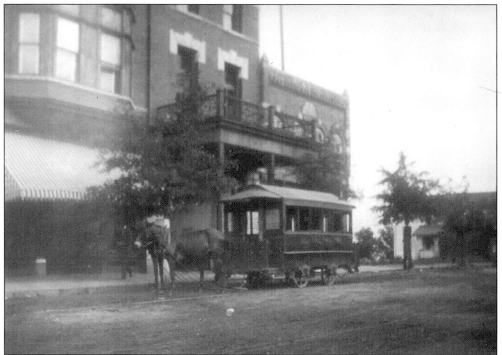

The mule-drawn street railway car stands at rest before the brand new Fitzpatrick Hotel in May 1900. Trees, planted just after the Great Fire of 1895, were beginning to provide some much needed shade on the wide-open and dusty square. (Courtesy Washington Historical Museum.)

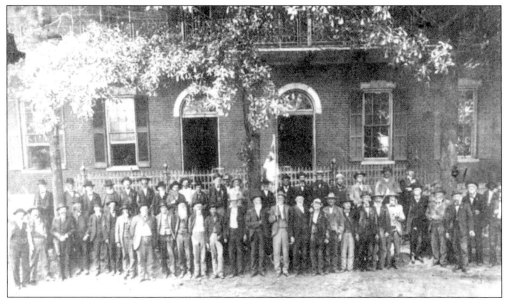

Assembled before the double entryways to the Old Bank Building (later the residence of Gen. B.W. Heard) are members of the John T. Wingfield Camp of the United Confederate Veterans. Situated at the upper end of the square, across Court Street from the 1817 courthouse, the Old Bank was a cherished symbol of the "Lost Cause."

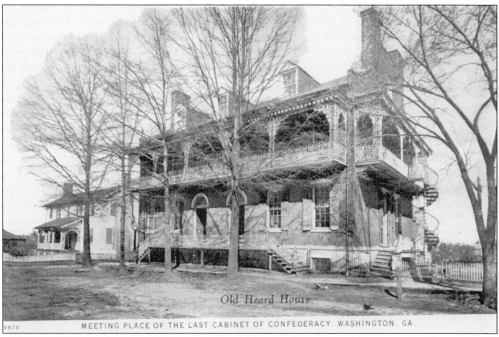

Following the War between the States, the old Bank of the State of Georgia building was sold to Gen. Benjamin W. Heard for use as a private residence. General Heard added the ornate ironwork, which brought a distinctive character to the historic structure. At the left is the 18th-century frame dwelling built by John Burch, secretary and aide to Gov. John Clark. (Courtesy Mary Willis Library.)

Panorama of Public Square, Washington, Ga.

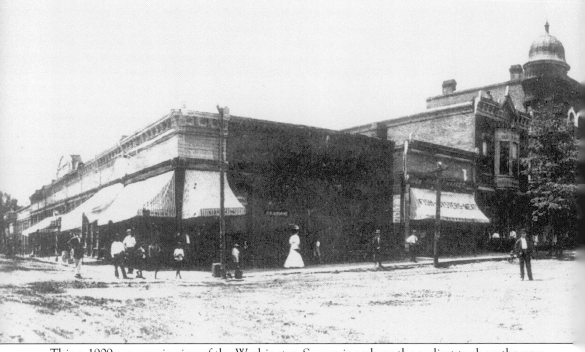

This c. 1909 panoramic view of the Washington Square is perhaps the earliest to show the new Confederate monument raised that year. At the far left is the Benson block, an inviting group of shops and small stores erected after the 1895 fire. The second storefront left from the corner

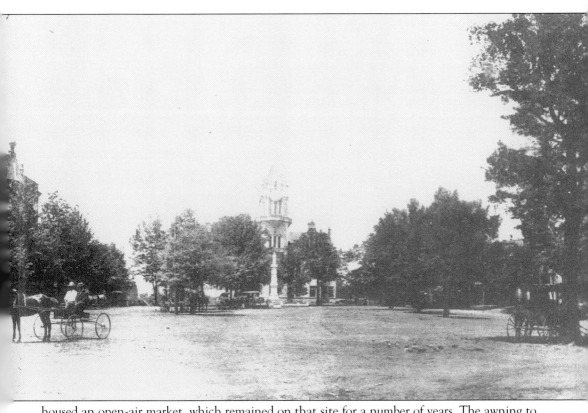

housed an open-air market, which remained on that site for a number of years. The awning to the right of the corner building advertises "Fish—Oysters—Meats."

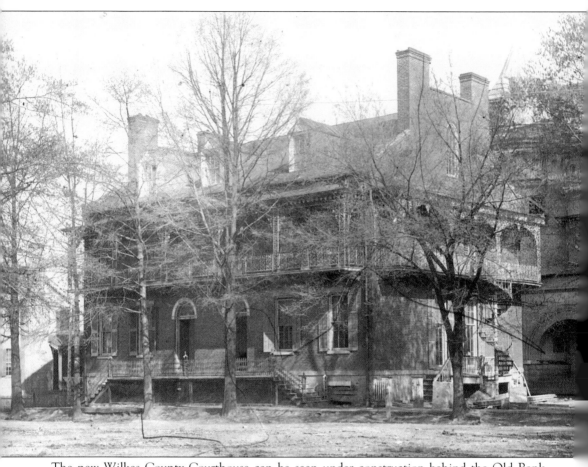

The new Wilkes County Courthouse can be seen under construction behind the Old Bank Building (Heard House) in this 1904 photograph. The scaffolding at the extreme right was set in place to erect the clock tower.

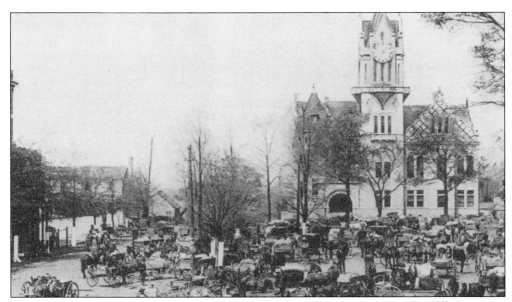

The new courthouse, too, witnessed Sale Days and Saturdays that continued to fill the square with wagons, mules, goods for trade, and people from all over the region. This 1906 view shows the new structure prior to the placement of the Confederate monument.

The monument memorializing Wilkes County's Confederate soldiers was placed in a prominent position on the square in the spring of 1908, and formally dedicated on April 27. McNeel Marble Company of Marietta, GA, crafted the monument. In his dedicatory speech that day, Garnett Andrews Green remarked, "Posterity, as it gazes upon this beautiful shaft, will not remember the toil, the strife, the bitterness of war—they will only remember the love, the heroism, the sacrifice of a lost cause." (Courtesy Mary Willis Library.)

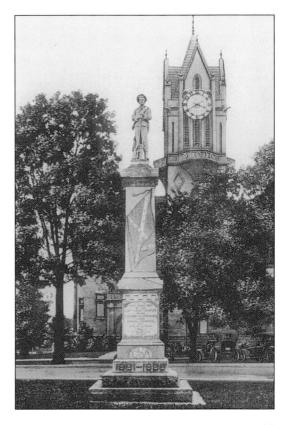

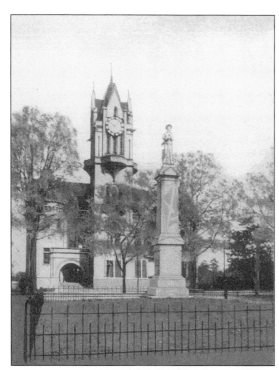

This early view of the courthouse and Confederate monument shows the iron fence that was placed around the perimeter of the marker in February 1916. The ironwork has long since been removed from the square, but still remains as fencing at a private residence on South Alexander Avenue. (Courtesy Mary Willis Library.)

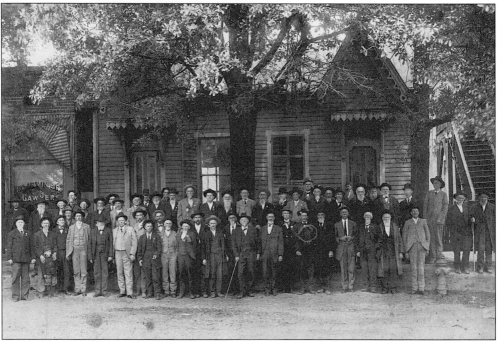

A group of Confederate veterans gathers on the east side of the square. At left is the brick law office of I.T. Irvin Jr., while the stairs at right lead up to the Masonic Hall. The residence at center rear was torn down some time before 1903. The gentleman with the cane at front row center is William Thomas Fluker Jr. (1845–1911), who served with the Crawfordville Home Guard and surrendered at Appomattox. (Courtesy Henry Harris Jr.)

Three
ECONOMIC VENTURES

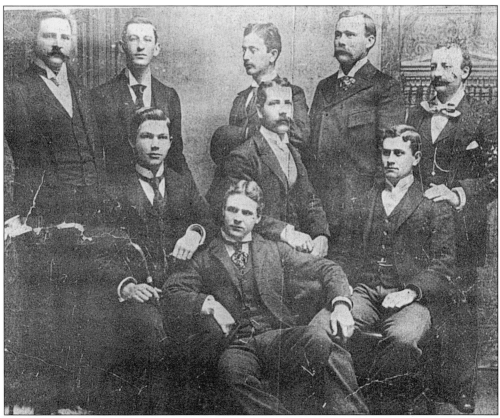

Washington was blessed in the last quarter of the 19th century with an active group of young businessmen who kept the community involved and progressive. Posing for this c. 1885 image, from left to right, are the following: (front row) Ollie Smith; (middle row) Ed Markwalter, Joseph Parantha, and Frank Callaway; (back row) unidentified, Abraham Franklin, Joel Latimer, J.R. Dover, and Harry O'Neill. (Courtesy Mary Willis Library.)

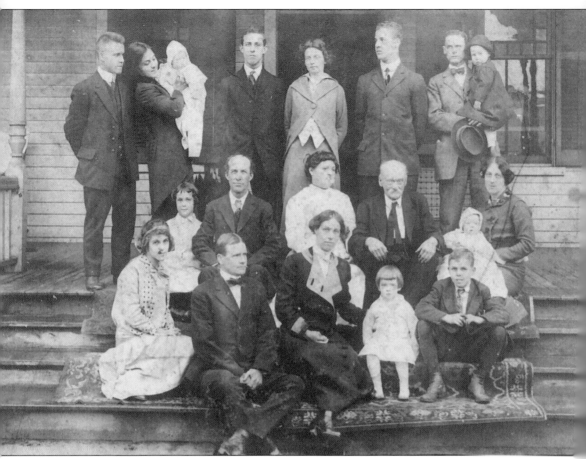

One of Washington's most enterprising young entrepreneurs in the rebuilding years after the War between the States was William Theophilus Johnson. Beginning as a clerk in German immigrant John Stummer's hardware store, Johnson went on to establish his own hardware business after Stummer's death. To that he added a dry goods and furniture store, along with a manufacturing company and building materials supply. In 1899 he erected a fashionable hotel, and by World War I his business "empire," the W.T. Johnson Company, stretched the entire block from Robert Toombs Avenue to Liberty Street. A deeply religious man, he was an ardent Baptist and trustee for Shorter College. In this family portrait from Christmas 1913, he is in the second row, second from the left. (Courtesy Mrs. A.D. Duggan.)

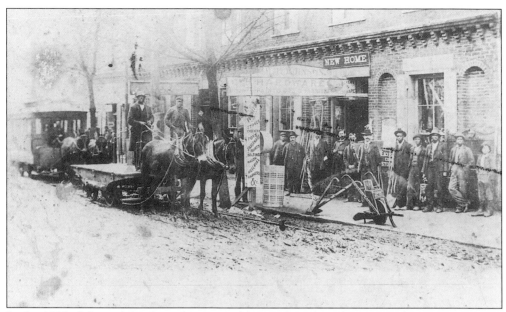

In the 1880s, Johnson's hardware business sold everything from furniture to harnesses to toys in its brick storerooms on the south side of the square. (Courtesy Mrs. A.D. Duggan.)

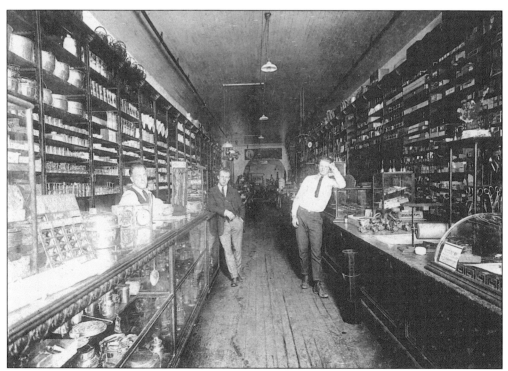

By the 1920s, Rochford and W.T. "Buck" Johnson and Eddie Blackmon (pictured from left to right) were clerks in W.T. Johnson Company's quarters, which rivaled urban department stores in quality and quantity of goods. (Courtesy Mrs. A.D. Duggan.)

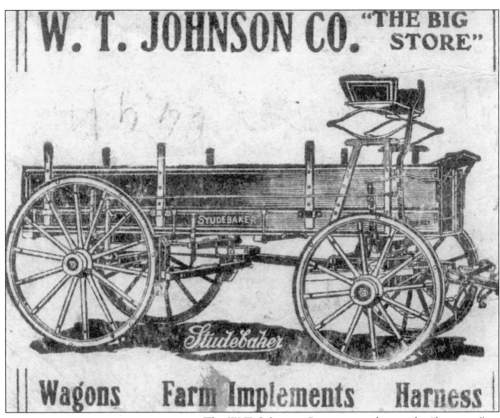

The W.T. Johnson Company truly was the "big store" in Washington, selling everything from corset stays to Studebaker wagons. (Courtesy C.M. Willingham.)

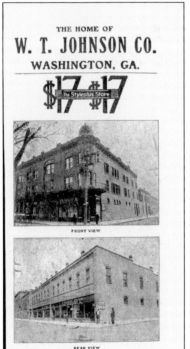

The store extended the entire block of Jefferson Street. Carriages, wagons, and furniture had their repository at the rear of the building, while the dry goods store was at the front. There was a hotel on the top two floors, and even a Chinese laundry midway on the Jefferson Street side in the days before World War I. (Courtesy C.M. Willingham.)

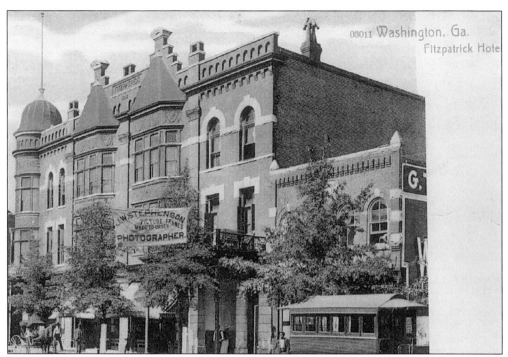

The Hotel Fitzpatrick, developed by John Fitzpatrick using architectural renderings by James W. Golucke, saw work begin in the heat of the summer of 1898. Various delays, including a workers' strike, prevented the hotel's opening until March 1, 1900. Far more elaborate than the Johnson Hotel, it boasted five large furnaces, an elevator, and an elegant ballroom. (Courtesy Mary Willis Library.)

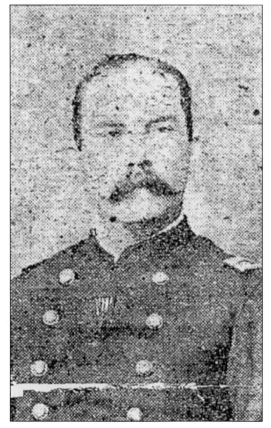

Capt. John H. Fitzpatrick was a leader of Washington's Irish-Catholic community and a determined businessman.

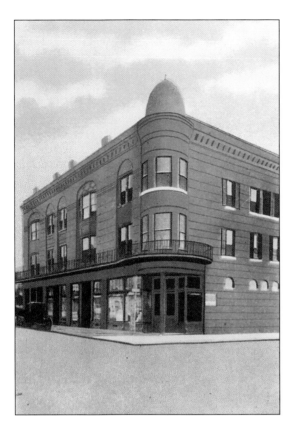

In mid-summer 1898, ground was broken for the Johnson Hotel on the old site of Bigby's livery stable with L.L Stephenson of Elberton as contractor. With both Johnson and Fitzpatrick realizing Washington's need for a quality hotel, the race was on to see who would complete a project first. Johnson's building was completed in record time, and was ready for occupancy by December 1898. (Courtesy Mercer Harris.)

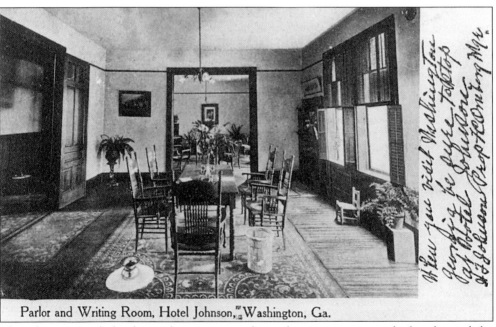

The Johnson Hotel also featured a spacious parlor and commons room, which enhanced the business's always strong reputation for hospitality. (Courtesy Mercer Harris.)

A third hotel was erected in Washington near the depot and was completed by 1899. Designed and built by Edward F. Barrows and named for him, the Barrows House was a "modern and efficient" hotel intended for the many "drummers" (traveling salesmen) who were frequently visiting Washington via the Georgia Railroad's "Picayune." Barrows was a trained architect who assisted in the construction of the monumental Atlanta Penitentiary.

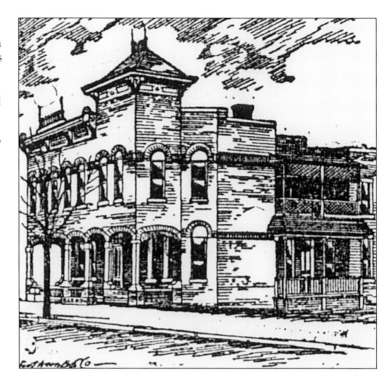

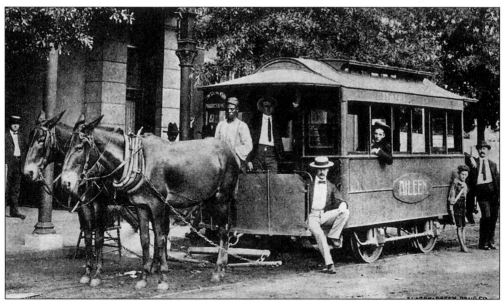

Transportation from the depot to the new hotels was provided by Washington's own version of "rapid transit"—mule-drawn trolleys that made several trips daily. Here, the "Aileen" rests before the entrance to the Fitzpatrick Hotel. (Courtesy Mercer Harris.)

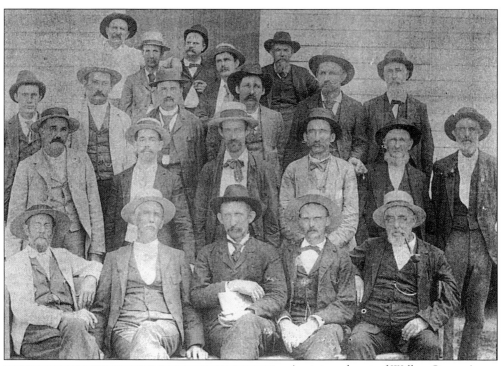

Official Premium List of the East Georgia Fair

Oct. 7 to 11 **1919** Barnett Park

 Washington Georgia

W. FRANK LEE

"Store of Many Departments"

Headquarters for FAIR Visitors

"On the Square"

Washington - - Georgia

An integral part of Wilkes County's 19th-century progress was the East Wilkes Agricultural Club, headquartered near Smyrna Church but including Washingtonians as well. The following members are pictured c. 1892 from left to right: (first row) C.A. Alexander, Simpson Booker, J.Luke Burdett, John C. Calhoun, and T.M. Meriwether; (second row) Vince Booker, Gabe Anthony, T.O. Holliday, Allen Kelley, A.C. McMekin, and Tom Mulligan; (third row) John T. Wingfield, L.M. Mitchell, R. Motte Smith, A.C. McMekin Jr., Jack Dyson, and A. Comer Barnett; (fourth row) C.A. Garrard, W.S. Hellams, J. DuBose Hill, W.P. Harper, and W.G. Tatom. (Courtesy Mary Willis Library.)

The East Georgia Fair was both an economic and social "happening" for autumn days during much of the early 20th century. This catalog celebrates the 1919 fair, which saw almost 9,000 patrons come through the turnstiles.

Moore's Mill was situated on Little River just off the road from Washington to Raytown. Pictured from left to right are Laura Mansfield Bell, Ruth Mansfield Ivey, Sarah Elizabeth Mansfield, Patrick Hugh Mansfield, and Mr. and Mrs. Jim Woodruff. (Courtesy Mrs. John H. Ivey.)

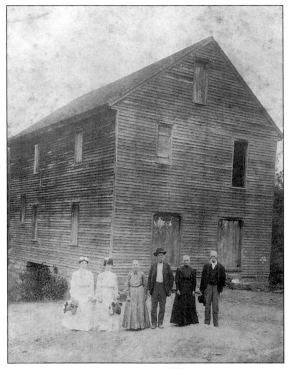

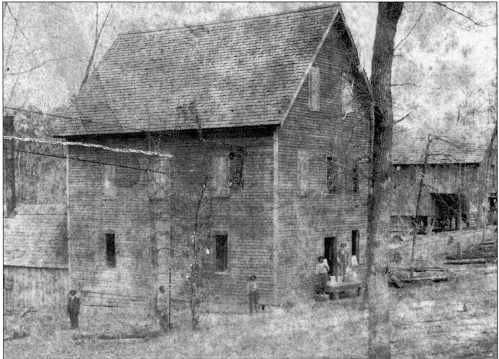

Edward Augustus Barnett was a major landowner and entrepreneur in the late 19th and early 20th centuries. A small settlement surrounded his mill a few miles west of Washington on Lexington Road in this 1885 photograph. (Courtesy estate of Mrs. Mary F. Barnett.)

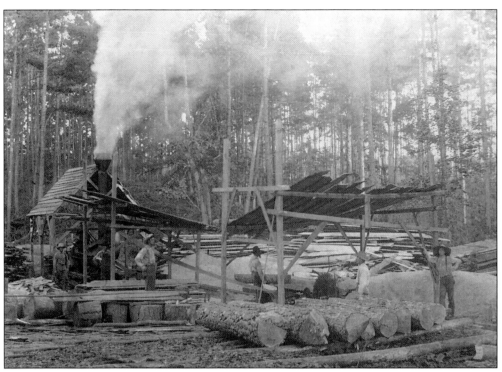

For over a century, timber and logging operations have provided employment and economic benefits for Wilkes County. In 1906, Robert Henry Johnson set up his sawmill on Tom Walton Road between Long Creek and Clark's Creek in the northern part of the county. Steam power was used to saw the often massive logs. Shown here, from left to right, are Ming Owens, Pink Johnson, Harry Walton, Will Booker, Bob Johnson, and Milton Johnson. (Courtesy Betty Slaton.)

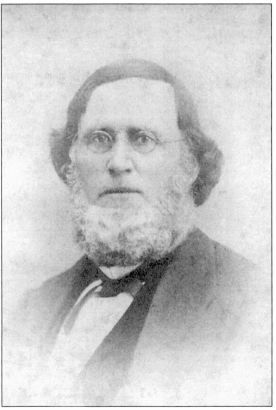

Robert Shand Smith (1815–1887) was a native of Charleston who moved to Washington in 1852. He was involved in a number of local business interests, and became the Washington agent for the Georgia Railroad, a position he would hold for three decades. In that capacity he was crucially important to the economic growth of the community. (Courtesy Mrs. John H. Ivey.)

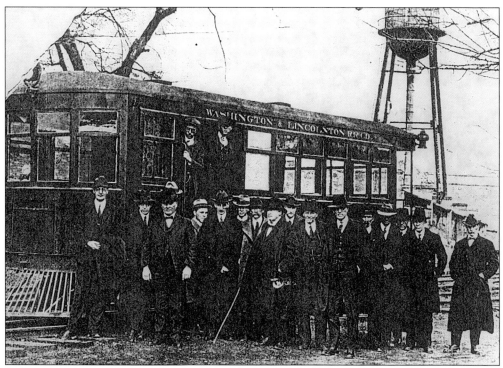

In January 1914, plans were begun for a railroad to link Washington and Lincolnton via Metasville and through the lucrative holdings of the Lovelace Lumber Company. Under President J.R. Dyson the line had been completed to Lovelace by October 1916. Lack of finances plagued its operation but it did actually connect with Lincolnton, only to fail during the Depression. Shown here in its more halcyon days, its founding fathers proudly stand beside the rail car at the Washington track interchange near present Wills Memorial Hospital. (Courtesy Mary Willis Library.)

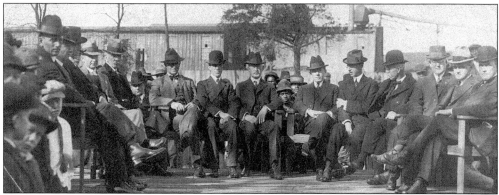

The Washington and Lincolnton Railroad was a grand proposal that sought economic revival for the area. The following stockholders are shown on the dais in 1916, from left to right: M.P. Pope, Marcus Pharr, J.M. Pitner, Luke Faver, Dr. T.B. Lovelace, General Manager M. Mason, Will Wynne, W.T. Johnson, J.R. Dyson, I.T. Irvin, G.A. Green, E.A. Barnett, H.W. Quin, J.A. Benson, and F.H. Ficklen. (Courtesy estate of Mrs. Mary F. Barnett.)

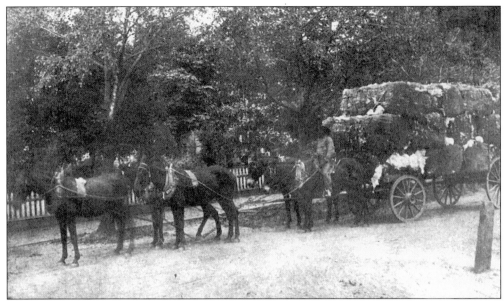

Cotton was the dominant cash crop for Wilkes Countians for well over a century. Whether prices were high or low, there was still a dogged determination not to yield to economic pressures to diversify. Only the devastation of the boll weevil finally brought planters to their knees and the cotton era to a close. Wagons loaded with bales were as familiar a sight on Washington's main streets as were the columned homes of the planters whose prosperity was due to the money the cotton crop provided. (Courtesy estate of Mrs. Mary F. Barnett.)

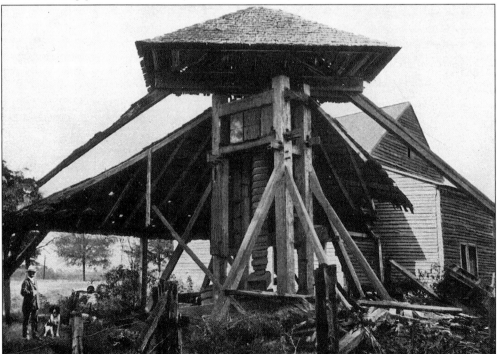

This cotton baler stood on the plantation of Robert Toombs and was used for decades. (Courtesy estate of Mrs. Mary F. Barnett.)

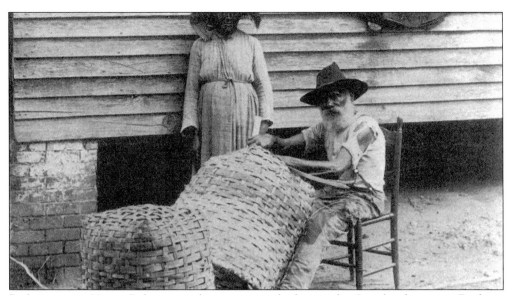

Basket weaver Henry Bolton completes a cotton basket at the Spratlin farm near Rayle in western Wilkes County. Standing behind him is his wife, Mandy.

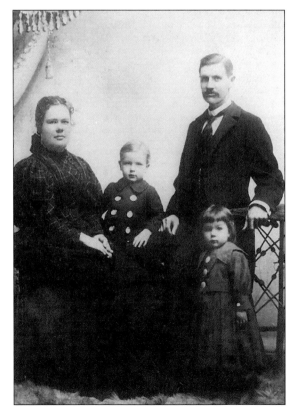

Dr. and Mrs. T.J. Wills pose with their children, Charles Edward and Tom, in this photograph taken by J.W. Goodman, who opened his gallery in Washington in November 1897. Dr. Wills was named first president of the Wilkes County Medical Society on September 29, 1905, and later served as president of the Eighth District Medical Association. (Courtesy Mary Willis Library.)

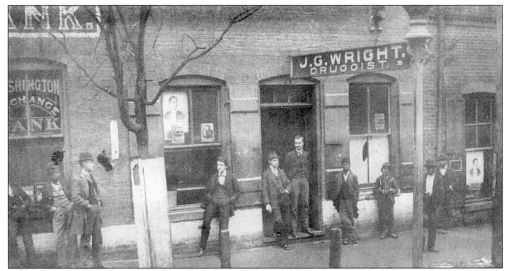

Downtown Washington was a bustling place, once boasting five thriving financial institutions. One of the earliest was the Exchange Bank, shown here in its Green block location next door to Dr. J.G. Wright's pharmacy. The pharmacy was a community landmark for over a half century. Dr. Wright is the hatless gentleman standing in the drug store's doorway. (Courtesy Mary Willis Library.)

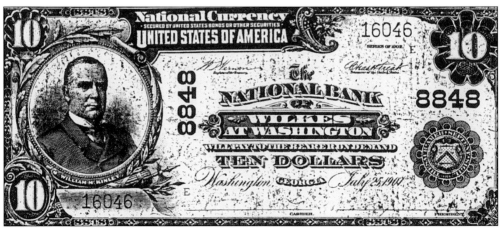

The Bank of Wilkes was nationalized in April 1907 to become the National Bank of Wilkes, and was allowed to issue its own currency. This $10 bill picturing William McKinley was issued July 25, 1907. The president of the bank was James A. Moss, and F.H. Ficklen served as cashier. (Courtesy Allen Brown.)

These two buildings were located on the south side of the square. The three-story brick Franklin building was the largest commercial structure in Washington during the 1880s, but was destroyed in the 1898 fire. Abraham Franklin was a popular and successful merchant for much of the latter part of the 19th century. The frame building at left housed Maryland natives O'Neill and Brother's dry goods and groceries. Anson King replaced this structure with a brick storehouse in 1892. (Courtesy Mary Willis Library.)

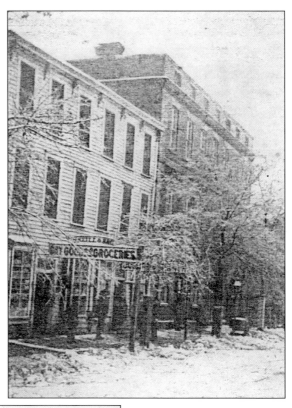

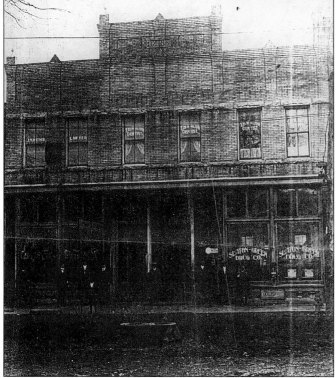

In 1898, following the devastating fire, Anson King erected this fashionable yellow brick commercial building on the south side of the square. Slaton-Green Drugs and Wootten's Dry Goods operated from the first floor, while attorney J.M. Pitner and dentist Dr. T.B. Walton had office space on the second floor. (Courtesy Mary Willis Library.)

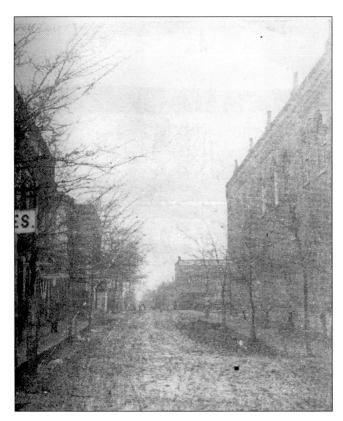

Looking west on Main Street in downtown Washington, the shop sign at the left is for Henry Cordes, watchmaker and photographer. An ardent Confederate, "Corporal" Cordes was instrumental in helping to organize the local Confederate veterans after the war. In the center background of this c. 1880 view is the frame structure known as "Bolton's Range," which housed a tinner, a grocery, and a saloon. (Courtesy Mary Willis Library.)

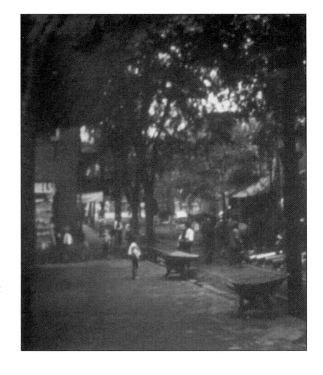

Downtown Washington was abuzz in May 1900 not only because of the solar eclipse but the paving of Main Street (now Robert Toombs Avenue) and laying of the "rapid transit" rails. The work crew has set down their wheelbarrows in front of the Johnson Hotel to mill about in front of John A. Logan's grocery across the street. The Opera House, a cultural and entertainment center for the energetic town, can be seen in the background with its overhanging balcony. (Courtesy Washington Historical Museum.)

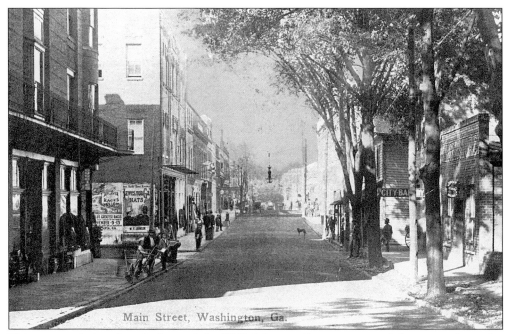

This westward view from in front of the W.T. Johnson Company toward the square shows the Singer Sewing Machine Store and J.B. Ott's Bakery at the right, c. 1911. The gaudy advertising signs are on the side of the Lyndon Opera House, which would be destroyed by fire in 1912. A hanging traffic signal is visible at the center. (Courtesy Mercer Harris.)

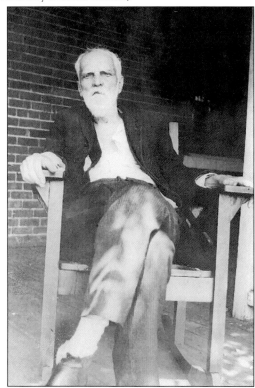

One of Washington's leading businessmen in the late 19th century was Rufus L. Foreman, whose dry goods business and partnerships with others, particularly Hugh Quin, made him a wealthy man. However, like most area merchants, such fortunes were both gained and lost over the years due to the vagaries of economics. (Courtesy Mary Willis Library.)

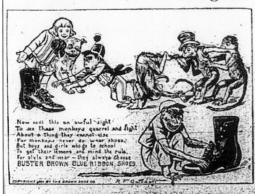

Phil Rosenberg arrived in Washington from Clayton, AL, in August 1908 to open his dry goods store. In 1916, Rosenberg sold his business to Ike Sabel and contemplated constructing a three-story office building just north of the Fitzpatrick Hotel. This effort came to nought and Rosenberg left Washington in 1919. While here, he was an enterprising and innovative businessman with several high-profile promotions such as Buster Brown and his dog Tige, celebrated performers of that first decade of the 20th century.

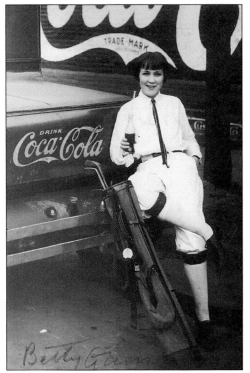

As ubiquitous as cotton bales in early-20th-century Washington-Wilkes was that "pause that refreshes"—Coca-Cola. In November 1907, Washington's Coca-Cola bottler, Thomas M. Nabers, erected a new bottling plant on Liberty Street. Nabers sold out in 1913 for a substantial sum that included bottling and distribution rights for Wilkes and five adjacent counties. By the mid-1920s, when "Calendar Girl" Betty Gunn visited town, I.W. Jones was the plant manager.

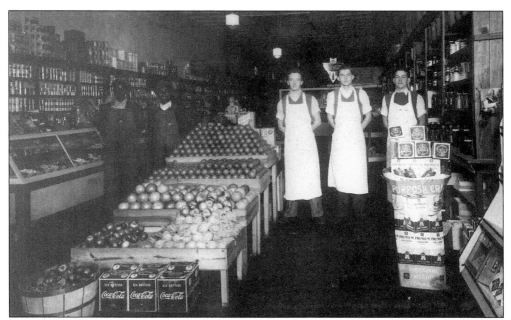

Armour's Grocery on the square was an active place in the years around World War II. Whether the trade was drive-up, walk-in, or home delivery, the store provided fresh meats and vegetables, canned goods, and a wide variety of whatever Wilkes County families needed for their kitchens or households. Pictured here from left to right are clerks Robert Jordan, Johnny Tate, William Taylor, Marion Willingham, and W.H. Saggus standing in the interior of the building.

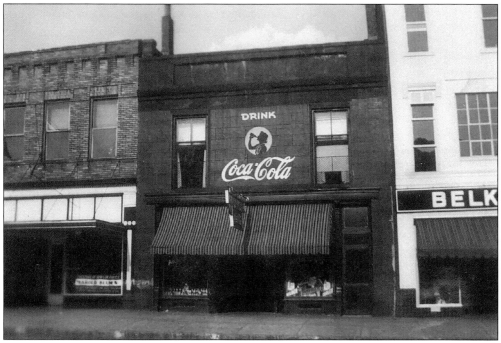

On either side of Armour's Grocery on the east side of the square were Harold Blum's dry goods store (left) and the Belk-Gallant department store (right).

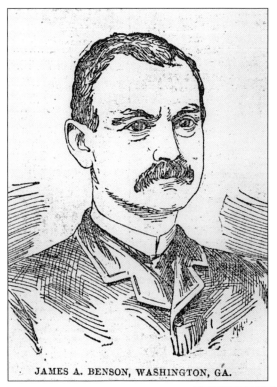

JAMES A. BENSON, WASHINGTON, GA.

One of Washington's most prominent 19th-century merchants was James A. Benson, a native of County Sligo, Ireland. He was a major supporter of the local Catholic church and invested widely in businesses from cotton buying to dry goods from the time of his arrival in Washington in 1870. By 1887 he was drawing over $130,000 a year from his various enterprises. (Courtesy Mary Willis Library.)

Mid-20th-century business leaders R.R. Johnson (left), Alfred Moses (left center), Frank W. Thomas (right center), and Nathan Tannenbaum (right) stand in front of the Washington Loan and Banking Company, a venerable institution that was a hub of economic activity. (Courtesy Mrs. A.D. Duggan.)

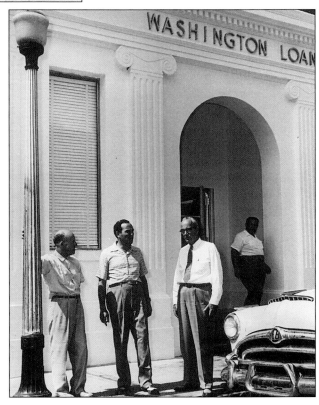

Four

HOME AND HEARTH

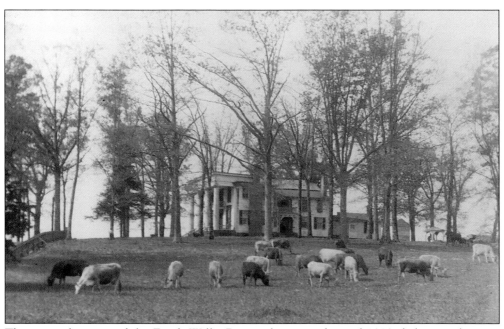

The pastoral setting of the Frank Willis Barnett home in the mid-1890s belies its closeness to town and the popular picnic area at the nearby mineral springs. Barnett was at one time pastor of the Washington Baptist Church and a strong proponent of scientific agriculture and diversification. (Courtesy Carroll B. Leavell.)

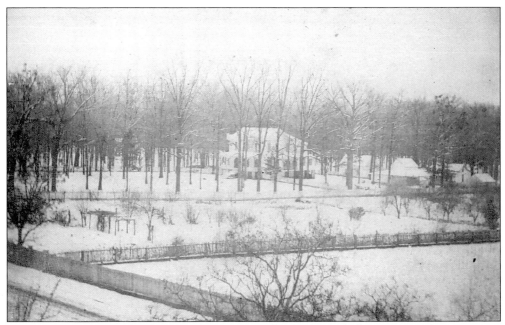

In January 1867, when the photographers Wren and Wheeler took this view, Washington was a compact community with most businesses and dwellings situated within two or three blocks of the square. Thus, the Samuel Barnett home (now the Washington Historical Museum) had the feel of a country residence even though it was less than a half-mile from the courthouse. Located in "The Grove," the structure also housed a respected private school of the era. Samuel Barnett was a highly educated and capable man who served as Georgia's commissioner of agriculture and was the author of a mathematics textbook. (Courtesy Mary Willis Library.)

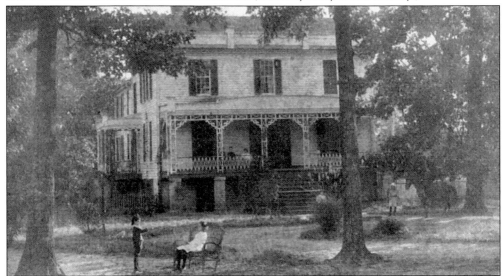

The family of Rev. Edward McKendree Bounds enjoys a spring day at "The Grove" in 1910. Reverend Bounds, one of Methodism's most prominent figures, was the author of inspirational books on the power of prayer that are still in print. He lived in this home from 1893 until his death in 1915. In the foreground are Paul Guerry Barnett and Mary Willis Bounds. At right in the background is another of the Bounds children, with a pony. (Courtesy Mary Willis Library.)

The daughters of Adam Leopold Alexander and his wife, Sarah Hillhouse Gilbert, strike a formal pose in this c. 1848 daguerreotype by P.M. Cary, who was practicing in Athens, GA, in May of that year. Harriet Virginia (1828–1910), standing, married Wallace Cumming, president of the Georgia State Bank. Louisa Frederika (1824–1895), seated, became the wife of Confederate major general Jeremy Francis Gilmer, chief of the engineer bureau.

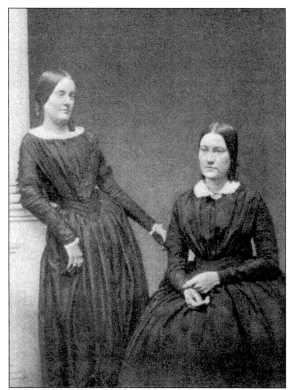

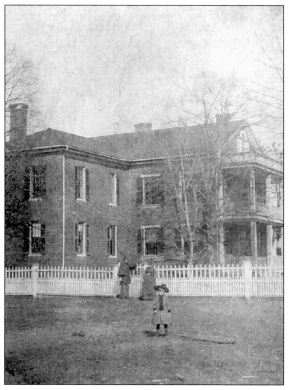

When built in 1808 by William and Felix Gilbert, this home was one of the first brick residences north of Augusta. Adam Leopold Alexander, a native of Sunbury, GA, and a graduate of Yale University, married Sarah Hillhouse Gilbert and enlarged the residence. The owner of the home in 1887, at the time of this photograph, was Charles Atwood Alexander, A.L. Alexander's youngest son, who is shown standing at the picket fence with his wife, Rosa Calhoun. In the foreground is their young daughter Carlotta. (Courtesy Mary Willis Library.)

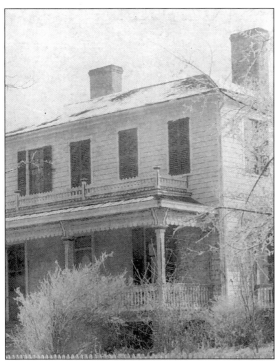

John C. Leitner first built this house in 1814, and Archibald Wingfield added the two-story portion after 1835. It was later the home of David G. Cotting, Georgia's secretary of state during Reconstruction. This view was taken in 1887, when the home was occupied by Enoch Binns. (Courtesy Mary Willis Library.)

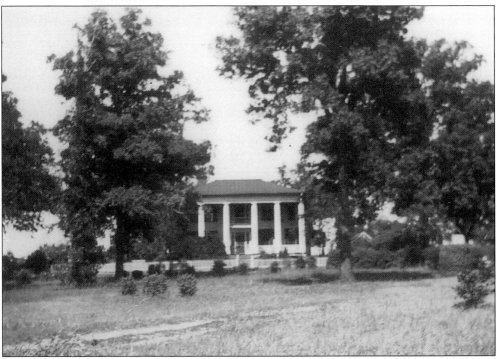

"Peacewood" was the center of a thriving plantation at Washington's northern limits. With a portion of the house possibly built in the 18th century, the primary structure dates from 1830, when Thomas Callaway owned the property. It was later the home of Dr. and Mrs. E. Boykin Cade, the in-laws of Georgia secretary of state Ben W. Fortson. (Courtesy Mary Willis Library.)

Garnett Andrews (1798–1873) moved to Washington in 1821 to develop a law practice. He married Annulet Ball on April 10, 1828, and in 1835 they purchased their beloved home "Haywood." Andrews became a popular and often controversial figure in Georgia politics, running for governor on the American ("Know Nothing") Party ticket and becoming an avowed Unionist. His witty, insightful book, *Reminiscences of an Old Georgia Lawyer* (1870), became a classic in its field.

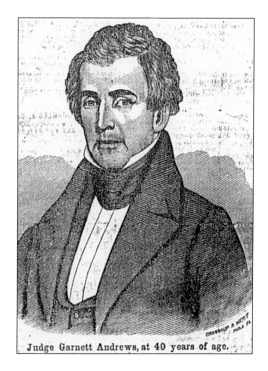

Judge Garnett Andrews, at 40 years of age.

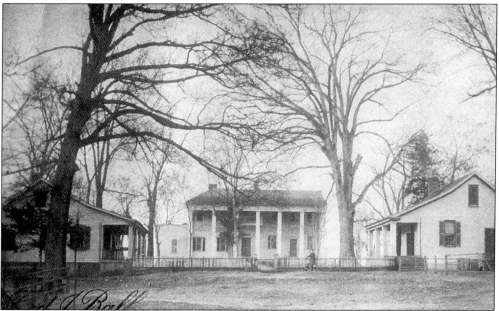

"Haywood" was witness to much fascinating history. The Andrews' daughters sewed the first flag for local Confederate sympathizers here in January 1861. Judge Andrews, despite his staunch Union sentiments, was always a gracious host to refugeeing Confederates. Both Blue and Gray soldiers used the spacious lawn to encamp in the waning days of the war and its aftermath. In May 1892, Judge Andrews' son-in-law, T.M. Green, supervised the demolition of the historic old house, which had been replaced by the Queen Anne-style "New Haywood" nearer the main street. Frederick J. Ball took this view c. 1890. (Courtesy Washington Historical Museum.)

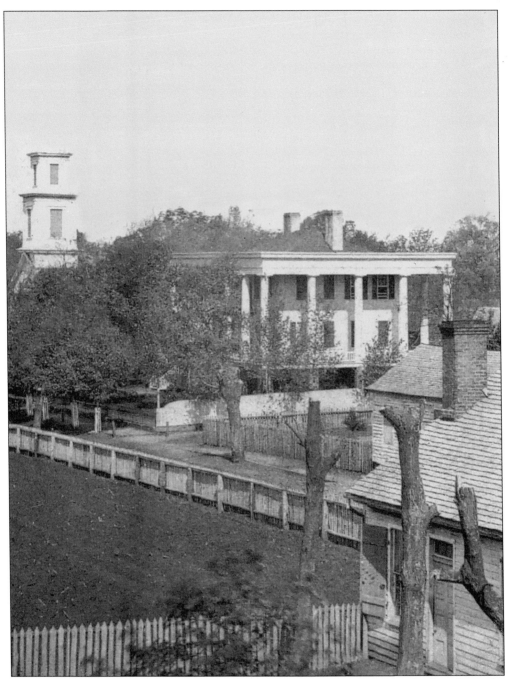

This westward view from downtown, taken by photographers Wren and Wheeler, shows the tower of the Baptist Church in 1867. To its right is the colonnaded home of its minister, Rev. Henry Allen Tupper, who in 1873 became head of the Baptist Foreign Mission Board. At the upper far right the roof and second-story windows of the 18th-century John Allison house are visible. Allison was a Revolutionary War soldier and his house was considered the oldest in Washington. It was destroyed in the Great Fire of 1895, which burned much of downtown. (Courtesy Mary Willis Library.)

This home was begun in 1832 by Dr. William H. Pope, but was best known as the residence of Rev. H.A. Tupper from 1853 to 1872. Tupper was pastor of Washington Baptist Church, and it was he who added the magnificent colonnade which surrounds the house. Reverend Tupper's granddaughter, Katherine Tupper, became the wife of Gen. George C. Marshall. The house is now a National Historic Site. (Courtesy Mary Willis Library.)

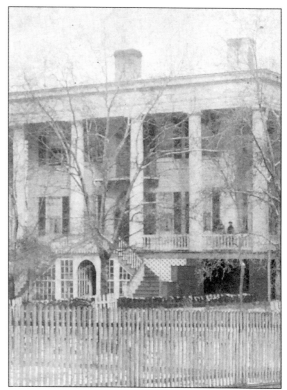

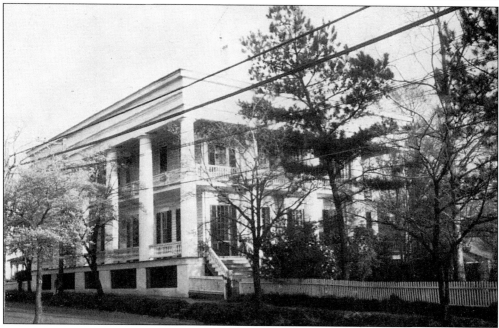

Supreme Court Justice John Archibald Campbell was born in this colonnaded home on East Liberty Street in 1811. Campbell was appointed to the court in 1853, and was a participant in the debates and decision in the Dred Scott case. Following secession he became an ardent Confederate.

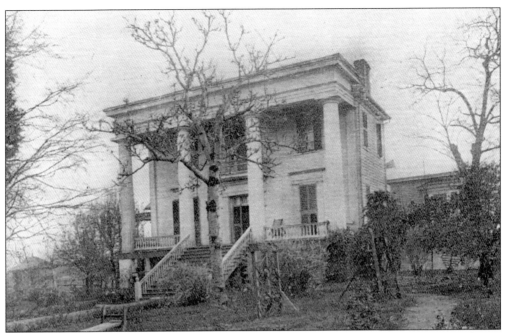

Probably no house in Washington is better documented photographically than the home of Confederate general Robert Toombs. Not only was his personality a dominant force in 19th-century Georgia, but the house itself was a fine example of antebellum architecture, having been expanded from its original small cottage of 1797 to a columned showplace. (Courtesy Mary Willis Library.)

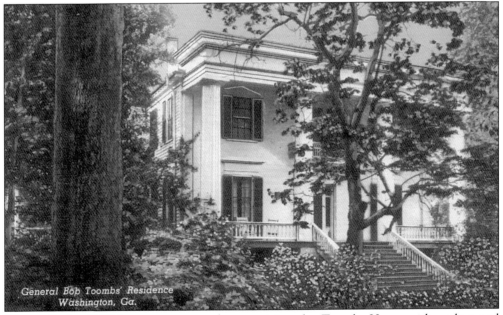

This stylized mid-20th century postcard romanticizes the Toombs House with azaleas and dogwood in bloom. Toombs' own exploits added to the mystique to the location, especially his daring escape from Federal troops in 1865 as he rushed from the back door to his waiting mare, "Gray Alice," while blue coats pounded on the front door.

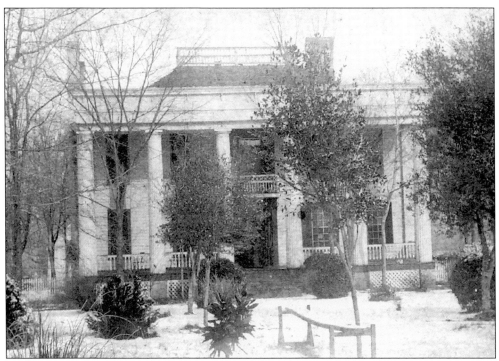

Unique among Washington homes because of its distinctive widow's walk was this dwelling on West Robert Toombs Avenue, built c. 1825 by Dr. Felix G. Hay. It was later the residence of Mrs. Epatha Rees Bowdre, who added the widow's walk around 1850. For much of the 20th century it was home to Mr. and Mrs. M.P. Pope. This view dates from c. 1887 and the ownership of William Alexander Pope. (Courtesy Mary Willis Library.)

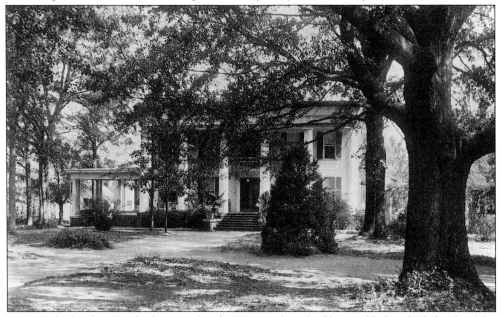

By 1919 the landscaping had matured and a porte cochere had been added to the left side of the M.P. Pope residence.

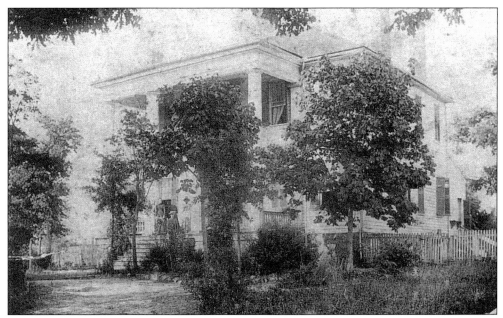

Located on Spring Street, the Stephen Pettus house was the site of much conviviality in antebellum days. It was purchased in 1881 by W.W. Simpson for his daughter Emma (Mrs. John A. Stephens). The family resided there until December 1888 when Mrs. Stephens, then a widow, moved to Atlanta with her children. The property was sold to Duncan DuBose. Shown on the porch, from left to right, are Janie Stephens, Mrs. John A. Stephens, Robert Grier Stephens, and housekeeper Aunt Malinday. Standing on the steps is Alexander W. Stephens. (Courtesy Mary Willis Library.)

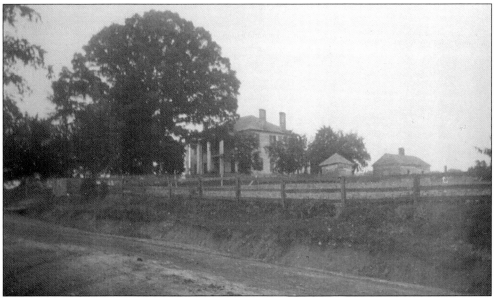

The DuBose house sat on the crest of a hill just east of Spring Street. In the large open field at its rear, the eclipse observation teams set up their equipment in May 1900. The house later was remodeled for use as the Washington General Hospital. (Courtesy Washington Historical Museum.)

The opening of the Grandview section subdivision in 1910 provided a new and convenient addition to Washington. It was located on the site of the observation post for the 1900 eclipse, just east and south of the Pettus-Stephens-DuBose home.

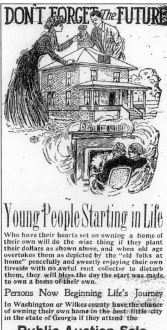

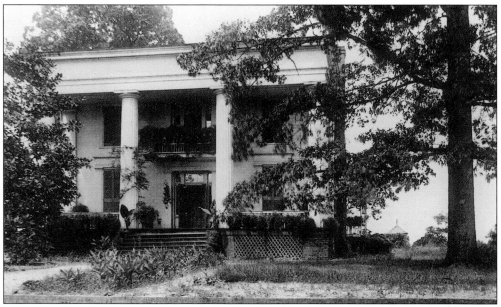

The seat of an active working plantation and an imposing antebellum home, this residence was begun on property originally west of the Washington town limits. It was adjacent to Effie Pope Park, an early community recreation area near the town's first water works. Daniel Chandler, state legislator and education reformer, erected the house in 1830. After the War between the States, it became the home of Charles E. Irvin, staunch Confederate and prominent civic leader.

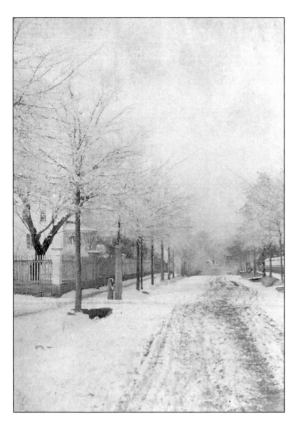

A mid-1880s snowfall is recorded in this scene of Main Street (now Robert Toombs Avenue) looking to the east. The house visible at the left is probably the dwelling Gabriel Toombs purchased in 1871 for his daughter, Julia Toombs Hardeman. (Courtesy Mary Willis Library.)

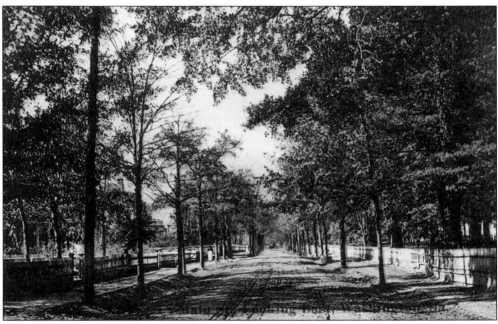

Thirty-five years later, when this postcard was issued, the view had changed little, but the neighborhood and its hospitality still thrived. (Courtesy Mercer Harris.)

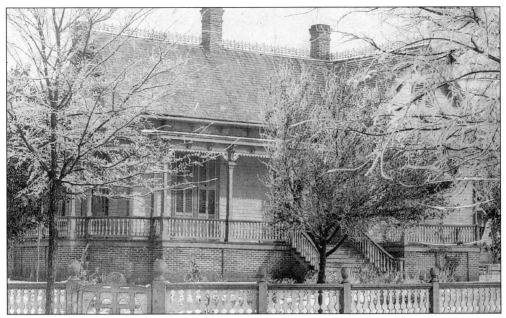

In the early 1870s a Victorian cottage was built for Thomas E. Fortson at this location, now the site of the downtown branch of the Farmers and Merchants Bank at the corner of North Alexander and East Robert Toombs Avenues. James S. Crouch and his family were later residents. In October 1910, it was purchased by R.D. Callaway, who had served as Wilkes County commissioner. The house was dramatically remodeled into a two-story colonial-style dwelling. (Courtesy Mary Willis Library.)

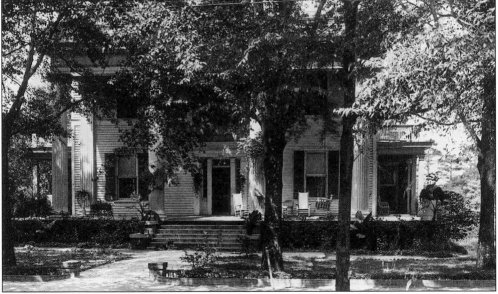

In 1919 the Gravure Illustration Company photographed a number of Washington homes for their series, *Art Work of Northern Central Georgia*. Among the homes featured was that of T.J. Barksdale on North Alexander Avenue. Barksdale was president of the Washington Loan and Banking Company, and in May 1909 had commissioned architect Charles Choate to add the Greek Revival colonnade to the front of his dwelling.

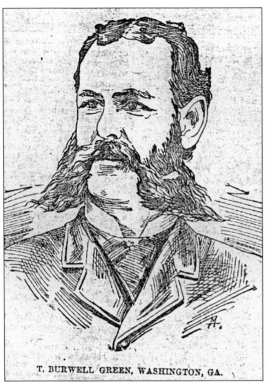

T. BURWELL GREEN, WASHINGTON, GA.

T. Burwell Green was a stalwart member of the downtown business community. He had been a Confederate soldier and then prisoner-of-war held at Camp Douglass, IL. After the war he remained in the Chicago area and amassed a considerable fortune in construction before returning to Georgia.

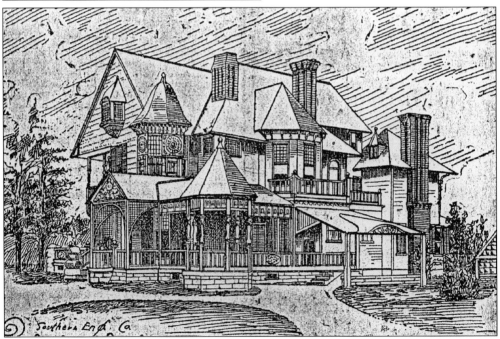

Green's home, which stood near downtown (where Fievet Pharmacy is now situated), was an outstanding example of Queen Anne architecture. It had been designed in 1887 by E.G. Lind, the architect of the Mary Willis Library, and was demolished for the construction of a grocery store in the mid-20th century.

Dr. Frederick Douglass Sessoms arrived in Washington in 1907 to begin his practice as one of the area's first African-American physicians. His services would span the generations and help to unite the races.

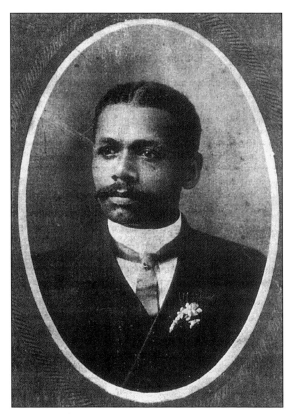

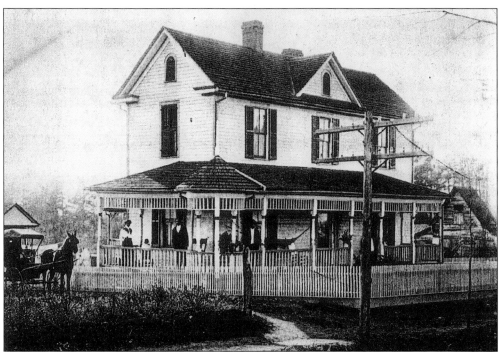

Dr. Sessoms built his new home on Lexington Road near the Shiloh Academy about 1908.

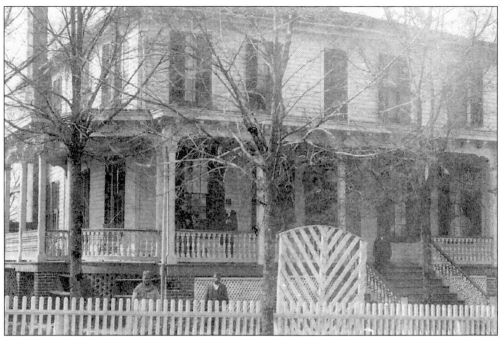

Begun in 1810 by William Prince, this was the home of Oliver Hillhouse Prince, codifier of Georgia state law and planner of the city of Macon. Called "Poplar Corner," it was the residence for prominent planter Alexander Pope until his death in 1864. His family later sold the property to Dr. Robert A. Simpson, beloved local physician, staunch Presbyterian, and Southern gentleman. (Courtesy Mary Willis Library.)

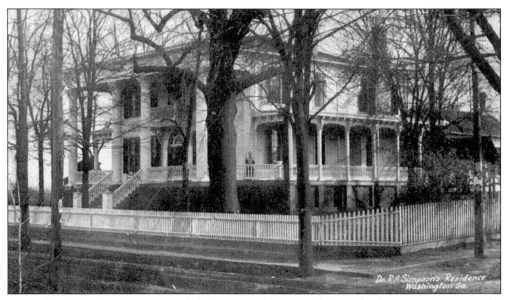

In 1905 Dr. R.A. Simpson removed the Victorian front porch from this home, replacing it with a stately Beaux-Arts Revival columned portico. A frieze of garlands was added by craftsman Frank Chafin and other fashionable improvements were made at the same time, turning "Poplar Corner" into one of Washington's most memorable showplaces. (Courtesy Mercer Harris.)

Five
EDUCATING THE PEOPLE

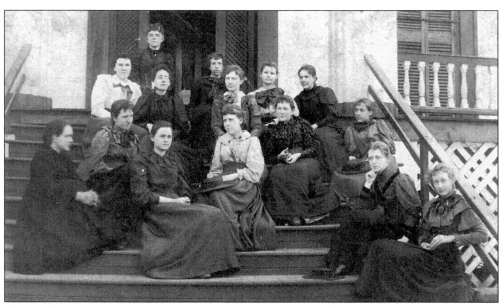

The Washington Female Seminary was one of the most distinguished institutions of its type for much of the 19th century. By the 1890s, it had ceased to be a boarding school, but the quality of its education was still high. Pictured is a group of ninth graders in March 1894, shortly before the Seminary and Male Academy merged to form the Washington Public School. (Courtesy C.H. Randall Jr.)

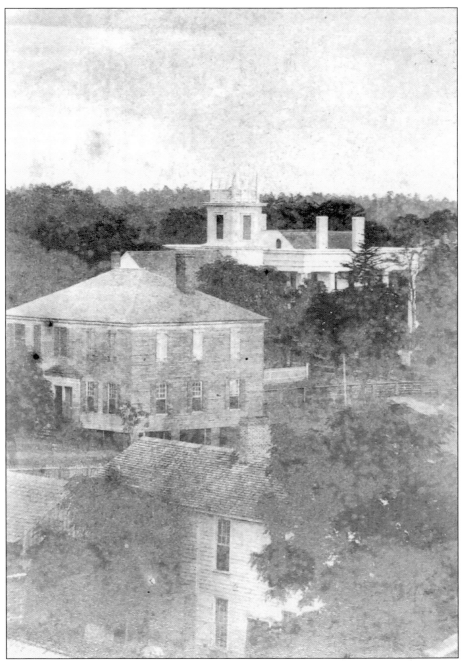

At the center of this c. 1875 photograph is the Washington Male Academy, a venerable Wilkes County institution that occupied this building from 1824 to 1897, when the new public school on North Alexander Avenue was opened. Federal troops commandeered and then ransacked the Male Academy in June of 1865. In the background is the steeple of the old frame Methodist Church, which was replaced in 1881 by a brick building (now the Masonic Lodge). Also seen in the background is the colonnade of the home then occupied by Benjamin F. Jordan. B.O. Bigby's house and harness shop are visible in the foreground. (Courtesy Mary Willis Library.)

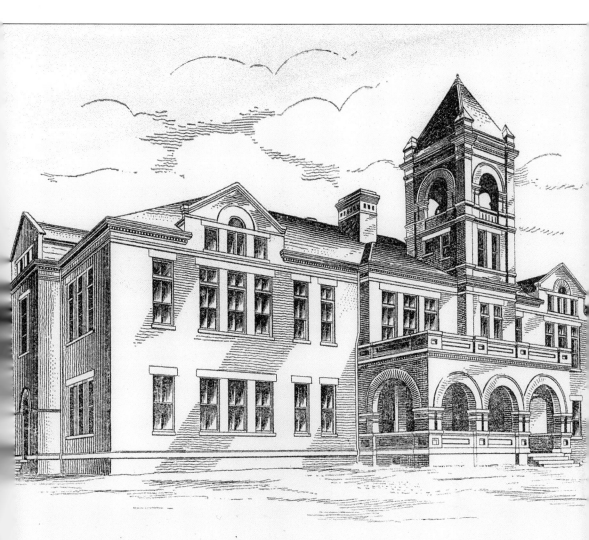

WASHINGTON PUBLIC SCHOOL BUILDING.   ERECTED 1897.

After over a decade of negotiations and false starts, a public school system for Washington had finally become a reality in the mid-1890s. The Male Academy and Female Seminary were phased out and gradually consolidated. Bonds were issued on July 1, 1896, for $15,000, and by March of 1897 this modern school building was ready for occupancy on North Alexander Avenue near the site of the old Seminary. B.S. Irvin was mayor and president of the school board while T.E. Hollingsworth was the first superintendent. It became the centerpiece for an educational complex that would later include another classroom building and an auditorium-armory.

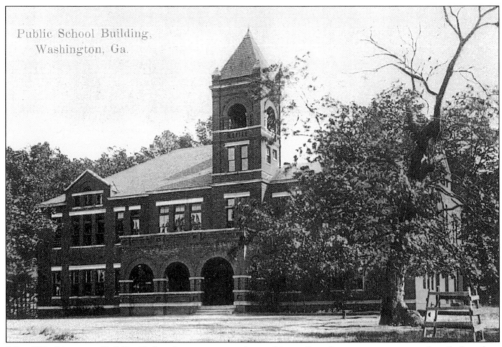

The Washington Public School was a popular subject for the penny postcards of the day. In the foreground, a piece of playground equipment for the smaller children is visible. (Courtesy Mercer Harris.)

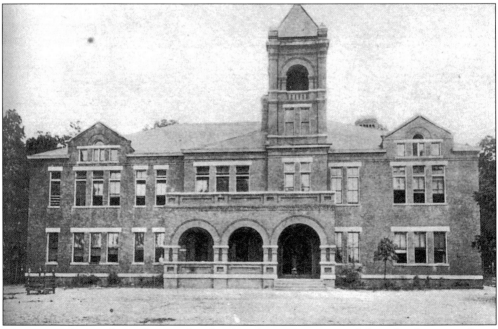

This postcard view from about a decade after the construction of the school was produced for distribution by Slaton-Green Drug Company on the square in Washington. (Courtesy Mrs. A.D. Duggan.)

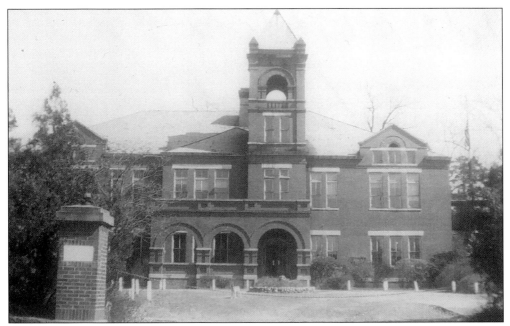

Efforts are underway through the North Alexander School Association to preserve this fondly remembered structure and use it once more for educational and community purposes. This 1920s view shows the bell tower whose ringing called generations of children to school. (Courtesy Mary Willis Library.)

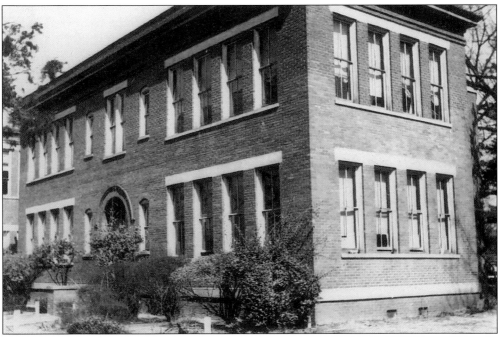

A growing school population brought on the need for additional classroom space, and accreditation was threatened because of overcrowding. In 1919 a bond referendum passed, 187-0, and work soon began on this two-story annex for the school. (Courtesy Mary Willis Library.)

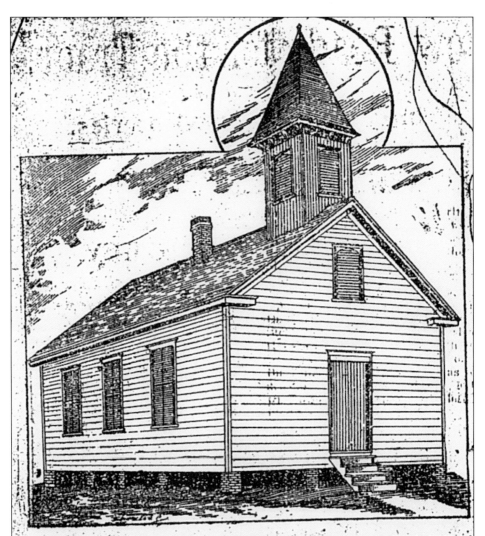

An important landmark of the African-American section of Washington known in 1907 as Freedmanville (and today as Whitehall) was the Wilson Chapel Presbyterian Church. It was supported by the "Northern" Presbyterians, although the local white church was also sincere in its efforts to assist. A fine school known as Hodge Academy, and headed by Wilson Chapel's pastor, Rev. J.R. Harris, thrived during this era.

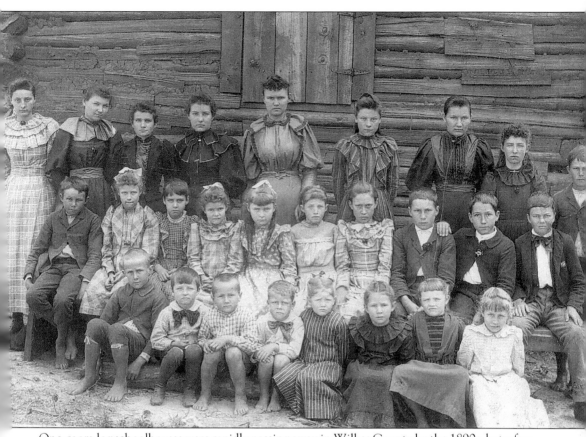
One-room log schoolhouses were rapidly passing away in Wilkes County by the 1890s, but a few, such as this one near Little River, still had their share of pupils. (Courtesy Mrs. John H. Ivey.)

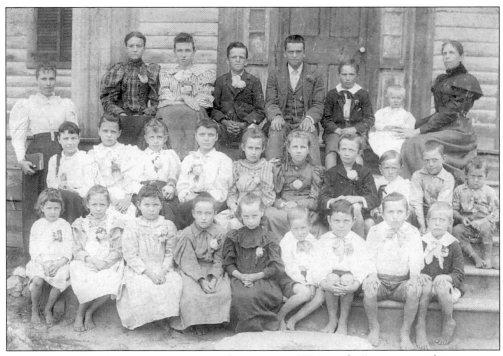

"Picture day" was a special time for students in the county schools. Notice the corsages and boutonnieres adorning each outfit. (Courtesy Mrs. John H. Ivey.)

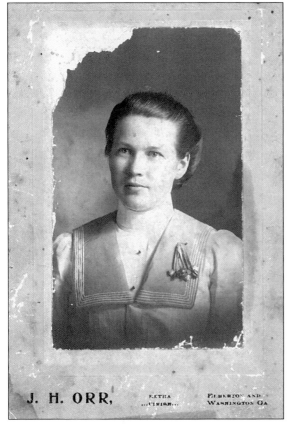

Photographer J.H. Orr established his studio and gallery at the new Heard Building on the west side of the square in November 1899. In early January 1902, he sold out to J.W. Stephenson. This example of Orr's portrait photography is of Elizabeth Roe (Lizzie) Strozier (1881–1939), daughter of Cyrus S. and Elizabeth Norman Strozier. In 1907 she was a teacher at Mt. Moriah School.

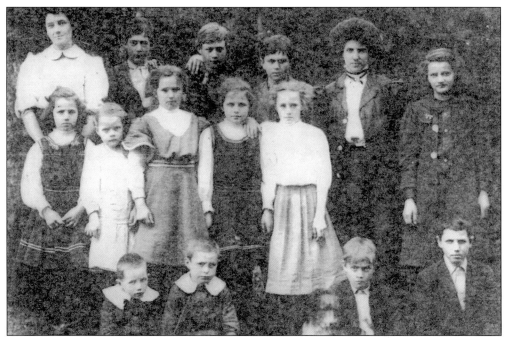

Big Cedar School, located in the Mt. Zion community near Little River, provided a fine example of rural teachers performing an admirable job of educating young people. This c. 1905 photograph shows pupils and teacher bedecked in their finest outfits. (Courtesy Mary Willis Library.)

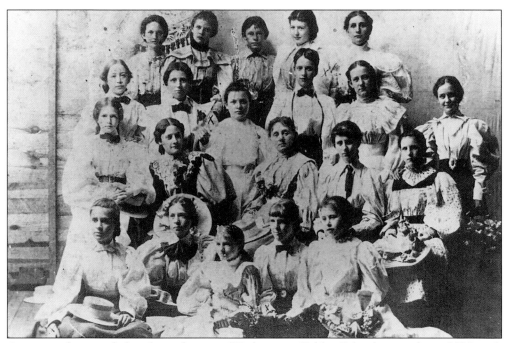

A group of young ladies from the new Washington Public School pose about 1898 with Miss Rosa Neeson (back row, center). Miss Neeson was, for over 50 years, a much-admired teacher in the schools of Wilkes County. (Courtesy Mercer Harris.)

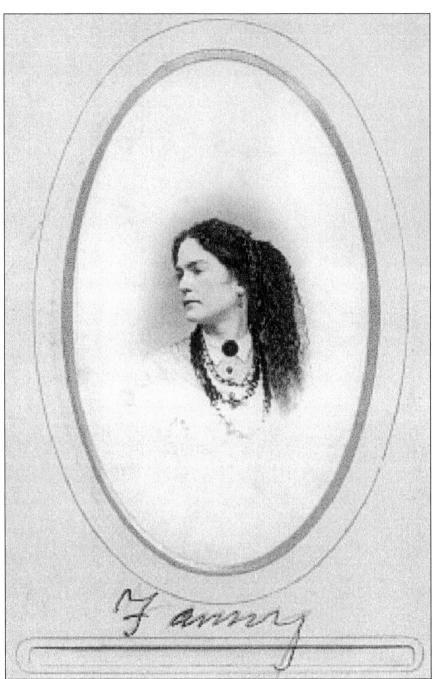

Eliza Frances Andrews, the daughter of Judge Garnett Andrews, was a zealous Confederate who, with her sister, sewed Washington's first secession flag. She also maintained a diary through those years later published as A *War-Time Journal of a Georgia Girl*. She became a respected teacher, novelist, and botanist, and was the first woman elected to the International Academy of Sciences. In the 1870s and 1880s she was both principal and teacher at the Washington Female Seminary. (Courtesy University of Tennessee at Chattanooga Lupton Library, Special Collections.)

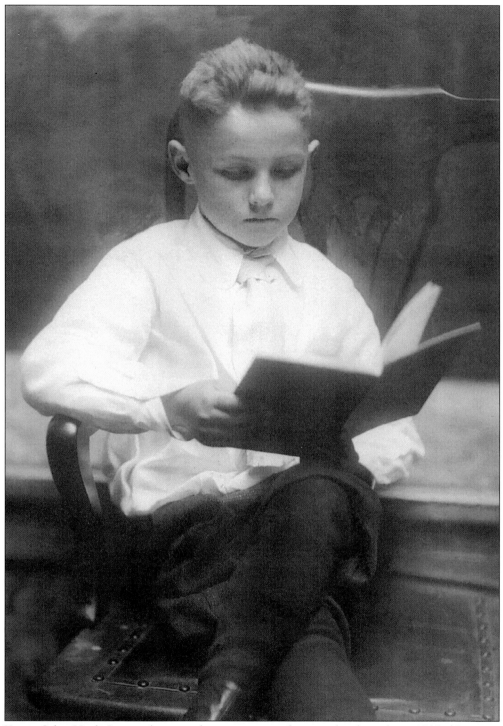
Young John Hugh Ivey strikes a studious pose in a photograph taken about 1918. (Courtesy Mrs. John H. Ivey.)

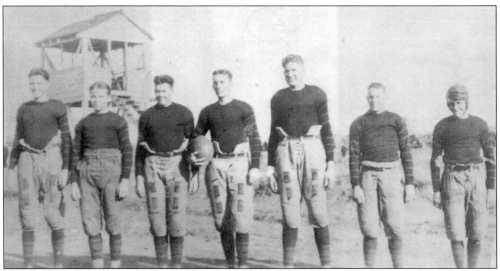

The 1922 Washington High School Bearcats were one of the finest teams in Northeast Georgia, finishing with an 8-2-1 record. The stalwart line, pictured from left to right, includes Joe Vickery, Joe Latimer, Henry Walton, Grady Cloer, Lucius "Tiny" Groves, Prentice Neal, and Malvin Vaughn. They stand before the coach's tower, which Rev. Homer Grice, Baptist pastor and coach of the team, used to observe his squad's practices. Note also the size and shape of the football held by team captain Cloer.

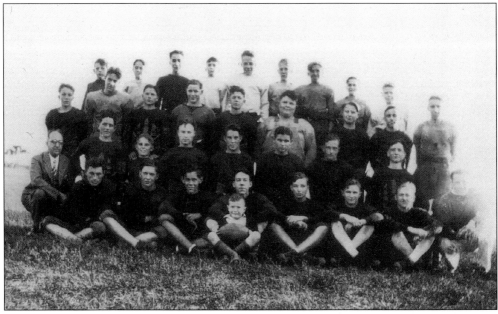

This 1928 Washington High football team was the first to become known as the "Tigers," having previously used the moniker of "Terrors" or "Bearcats." In the third row, sixth from the left, is Oliver Walton, whose nearly 300-pound frame would not fit into an existing uniform. He wore overalls until he could have a uniform tailored. (Courtesy Mrs. John H. Ivey.)

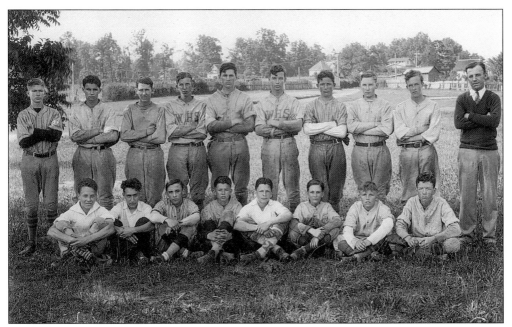

The Washington High School varsity and B-team baseballers line up for the 1929 season. Coach Hubert Tarpley (standing at right) supervised all the boys' sports programs for the school. (Courtesy Mrs. John H. Ivey.)

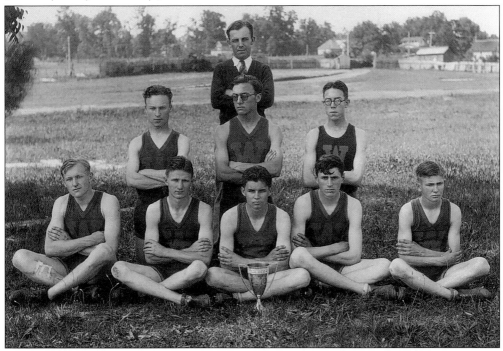

Champions of the 1929 Eighth District track meet were the Washington High "Tigers." Shown here are the following participants, from left to right: (front row) R. Motte Smith, Jack Eubanks, John Ivey, James Reynolds, and Leslie Jackson; (middle row) Charles Reynolds, Bruce Smith, and Clarence Garrett; (back row) Coach Hubert Tarpley. (Courtesy Mrs. John H. Ivey.)

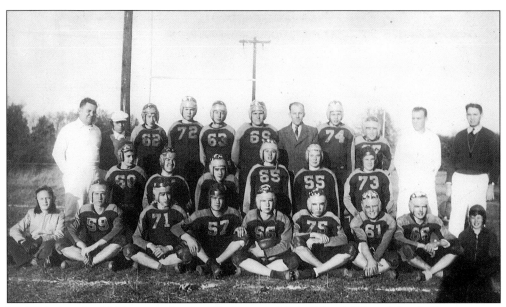

Highlighting the 1944 season for the Washington High School "Tigers" football team was a 32-0 Thanksgiving Day victory over arch-rival Lincolnton.

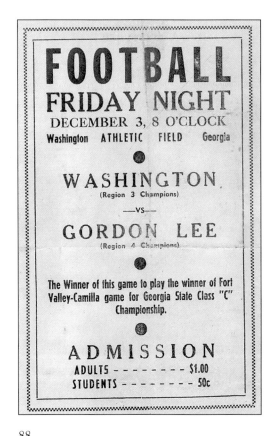

For over 80 years high school football has been a part of Washington society. First Washington High School and later Washington Central and Washington-Wilkes High Schools have brought championships and sports excitement to the whole community. Today, "Football Friday Nights" have become almost religious in their intensity. This 1948 contest was for the North Georgia Class C crown.

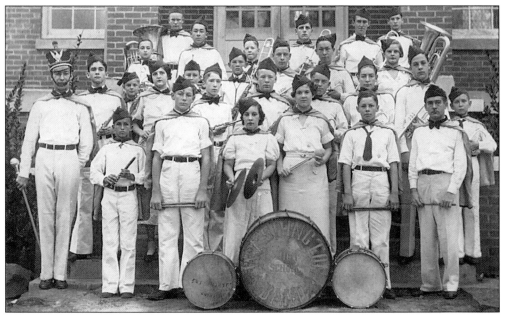

William T. Verran (front row, far right) was a Michigan native who came to Washington with the Barnett Brothers Circus. When the circus disbanded, Verran was left jobless in a strange southern town. A talented musician, he formed a band for Washington High School in December 1931. This organization has consistently been a source of community pride and has won numerous honors through the years. Drum Major L.G. Ray (far left) directed the 1933–34 Tiger Band, which was featured entertainment for the 1934 Georgia Education Association Convention in Savannah.

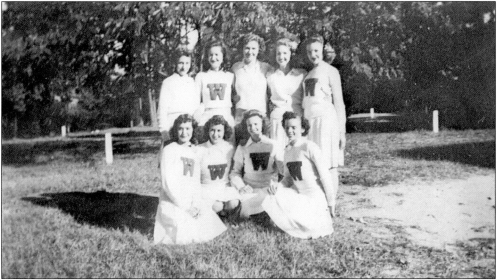

Cheerleaders for Washington High School first appeared in 1927, and by 1944–45, when this photograph was snapped, they were an integral part of the school program. Pictured here from left to right are the following: (front row) Frances Dent, Ruth Russell, Lillie Mae Jones, and Peggy Powell; (back row) Gloria Turner, Sara Sturdivant, Eugenia Forbes (advisor), Ann Fortson, and Bessie Louise McLendon.

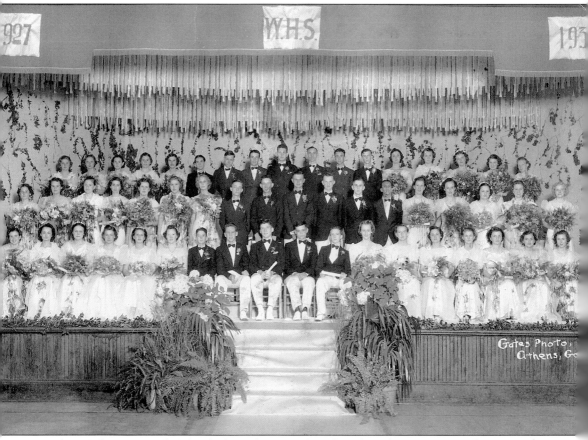

The Washington High School Class of 1938 gathers for a formal portrait on graduation night. The setting is the stage of the school auditorium-armory, which has now been converted into the Washington Little Theater.

Six
STRONG IN SPIRIT

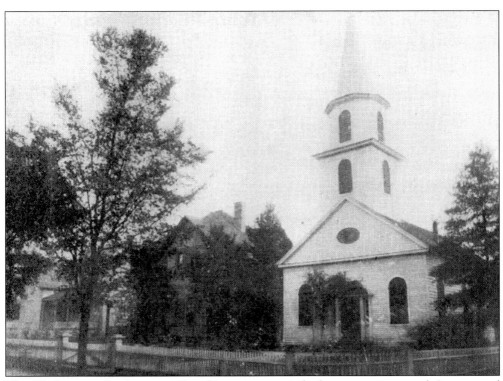

The Washington Presbyterian Church's congregation had its origins in rural Smyrna and Providence Churches that had begun about 1786. By 1820, services were being held in Washington. On July 29, 1825, the church trustees acquired the lot on which the present building was erected. The first pastor who preached from this pulpit was Rev. Alexander Hamilton Webster, who died an untimely death in 1827. His tomb is in the front foyer of the church. This 1890s view shows the church prior to the addition of its portico.

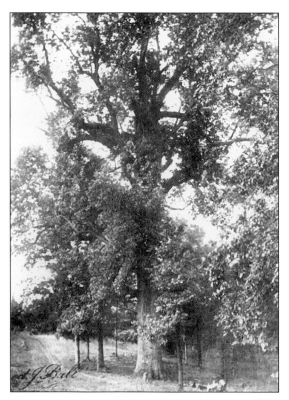

On July 21, 1790, John Springer, a native of Delaware who had come to Wilkes County in 1788 to establish an academy, became the first Presbyterian minister ordained on Georgia soil. His ordination occurred under a large poplar tree just east of Washington's downtown. The tree no longer stands, although a historic marker on Poplar Drive now designates the spot. This photograph was taken about 1890 by Frederick J. Ball.

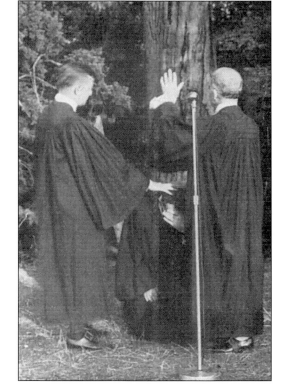

In October 1940, the Augusta Presbytery met in Washington to celebrate the sesquicentennial of Reverend Springer's ordination and, as part of the service, held a reenactment ceremony at the original site.

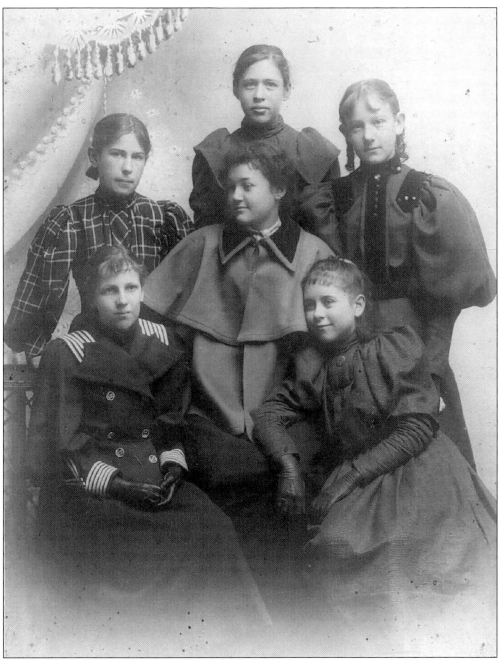

In 1895, as a Christmas present to their teacher, Ruth Irvin Foreman, the young ladies of the Washington Methodist Church Sunday School had local photographer J.W. Goodman take their picture. Goodman's studio was upstairs in a building on the square and featured a skylight to aid in his compositions. The young ladies pictured are as follows, from left to right: (front row) Kathleen Colley, Esther Lowe, and Sarah Quillian; (back row) Mary Irvin, Claud Ficklen, and Effie Wood. (Courtesy Mary Willis Library.)

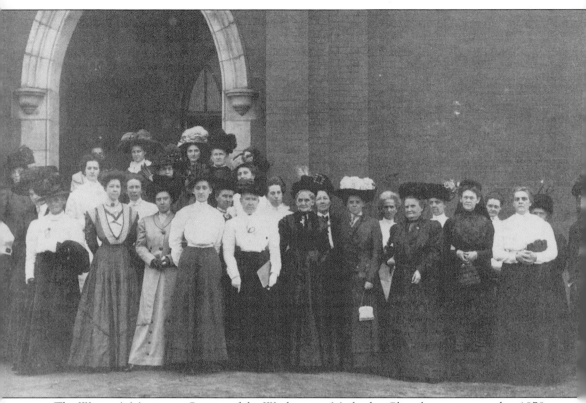
The Women's Missionary Society of the Washington Methodist Church was organized in 1878. These ladies have gathered shortly after the completion of the new church building in 1910 for a district Missionary Society rally.

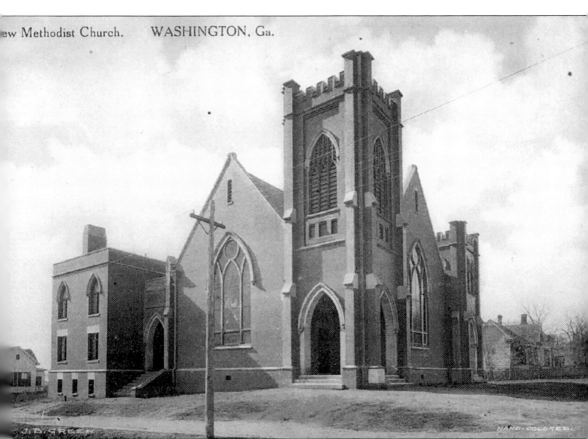

ew Methodist Church.   WASHINGTON, Ga.

The Methodists became the first denomination to build a church in Washington. Work began in 1820 on a Liberty Street lot purchased the previous year. In 1881 this first frame church was replaced by a brick building that served almost three decades. As early as the 1890s, Washington Methodists realized that their fast-growing congregation was outgrowing its East Liberty Street home. However, it was not until August 8, 1906, that the dream became reality. The munificence of devoted member Thomas C. Hogue provided both a lot on which to construct a new church and the financial gifts to bring the project to fruition. The pastor during the building program was Rev. H.J. Ellis. On July 17, 1910, the new church was finally dedicated in an impressive ceremony with Bishop H.C. Morrison in attendance. This postcard view featuring the brand new structure also shows at far left the residence of Phil Rosenberg, just completed in November 1909. (Courtesy Mary Willis Library.)

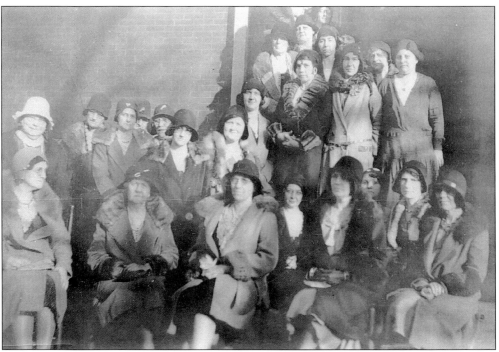

In the late 1920s the Ladies Sunday School Class of the Washington First Methodist Church posed on the steps at the church's side entrance. (Courtesy Mrs. John H. Ivey.)

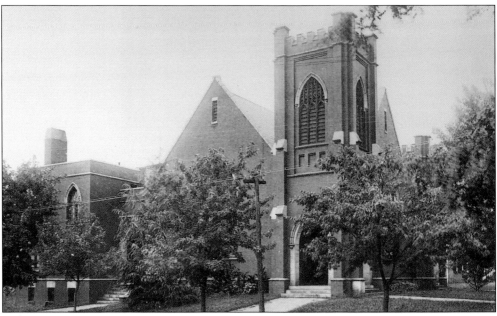

Landscaping provided a more elegant setting for the Washington Methodist Church by 1919. During the pastorate of Rev. G.S. Frazier (1917–1920), the first Methodist Men's Club in the history of the denomination was formed at this church.

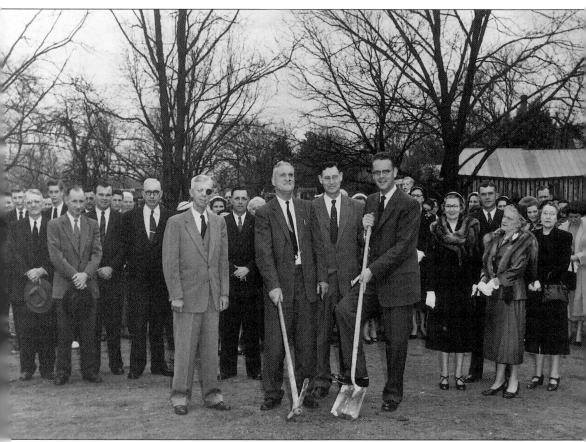

On the night of November 20, 1955, disaster struck the Methodist church as fire ravaged the building. Remarkable efforts by the volunteer fire department and Chief Rufus Rider saved the structure and its magnificent stained-glass windows. Following the fire, church leaders decided not only to renovate the existing facility but also to erect an education building. Pictured in the foreground, from left to right, are the prime movers for this project—Marion H. Barnett, James H. Blackmon, Rev. Max M. Whittemore, and L.L. Lannae.

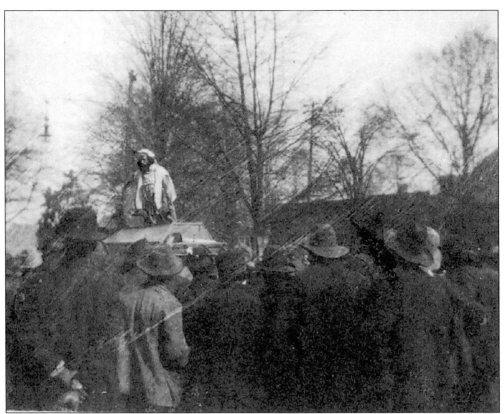
An African-American revivalist preacher known as "The Prophet" dazzled local audiences with his fiery oratory and spirituality during 1907. He set up his pulpit on the square.

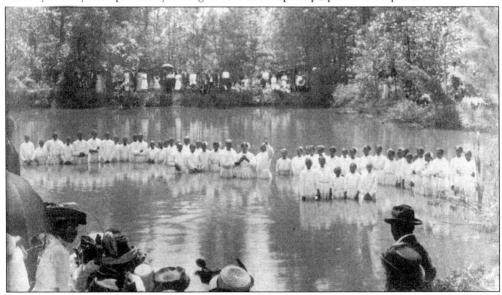
In 1913, Washington photographer J.W. Stephenson was present to record this baptismal service for New Salem Baptist Church. The minister, Rev. R.W. White, is at the center with his hand raised. (Courtesy estate of Mrs. Mary F. Barnett.)

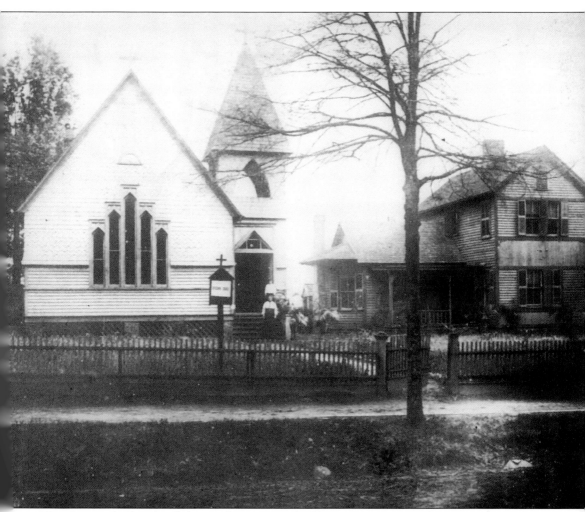

The Episcopal Church of the Mediator's new building was consecrated on June 21, 1896, although the final touches would not be completed until 1899. Construction on the adjacent rectory was underway by April of 1897. Rev. J.J. Lanier was rector from 1907 to 1910, the period during which this photograph was taken. (Courtesy Mary Willis Library.)

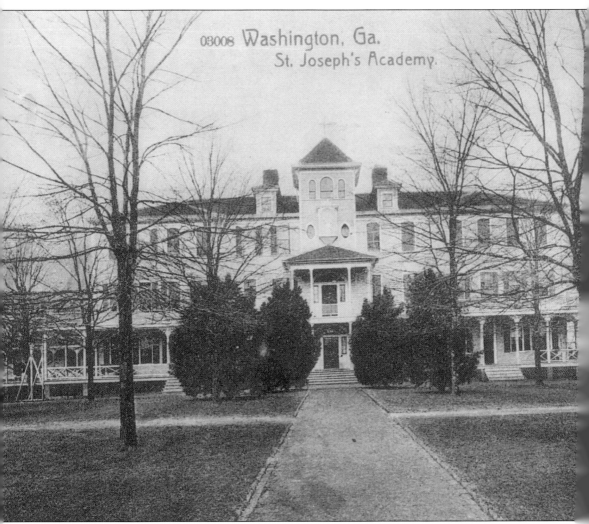

In 1875, Father James M. O'Brien was resident priest for St. Patrick's Catholic Church in Washington. Through his efforts and those of Diocesan Bishop William H. Gross, a house and 50 acres were purchased in January 1876 from the estate of Nicholas Wylie on Academy Hill, just west of downtown Washington, to establish the St. Joseph's Home for orphan boys. The residence on the property had once been home to revered Baptist minister Rev. Jesse Mercer. Assuming the teaching responsibilities was the Sisterhood of St. Joseph, and their convent was moved to Washington from Savannah. By 1877, the St. Joseph's Academy, a "Boarding and Day School for Young Ladies," had been developed in conjunction with the orphanage. Among the many girls educated there were the daughters of Joel Chandler Harris, "Uncle Remus," who was a frequent visitor to the campus. Numerous expansions made the structure a rambling hodgepodge. Following an 1898 fire, local architect E.F. Barrows designed a facility that would become the largest building between Athens and Augusta. On November 20, 1912, another fire devastated the Girls' Academy, resulting in a $ 75,000 loss and the permanent removal of the academy to Augusta. The orphanage, however, remained a local mainstay for another 50 years. (Courtesy Mary Willis Library.)

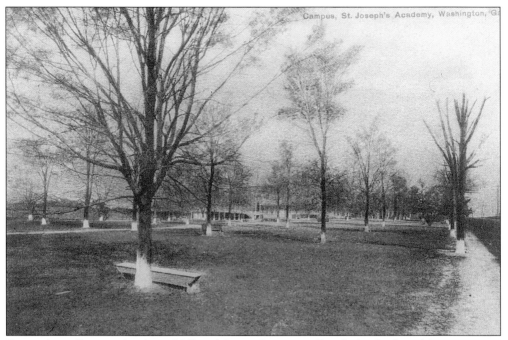
Situated regally atop Academy Hill and facing Lexington Road, the St. Joseph's campus was spacious and always well maintained.

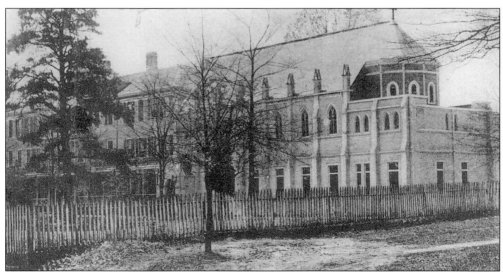
This side view of the structure emphasizes the expansiveness of the building, which housed not only the boys' orphanage but also girls' academy and chapel. (Courtesy Mary Willis Library.)

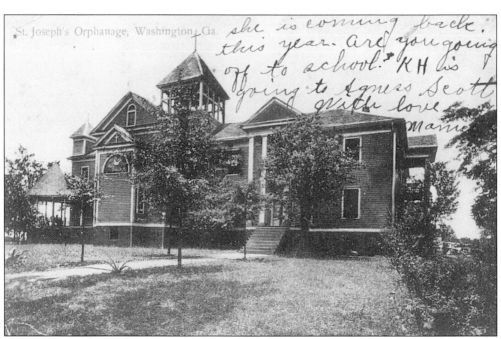
Another side view of St. Joseph's shows clearly how the original Jesse Mercer homestead had been incorporated into the overall structure of the facility. (Courtesy Mercer Harris.)

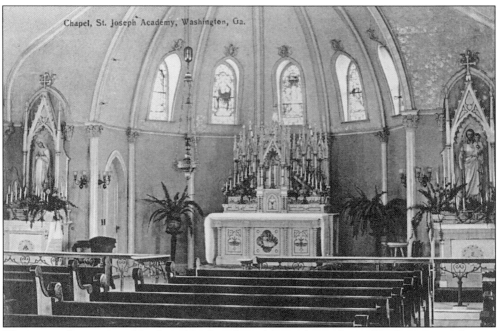
The ornate decoration of St. Joseph's chapel was like nothing else in Washington, and was a serene haven for the local Catholic community. (Courtesy Mercer Harris.)

The leader of Georgia's Baptists in the early 19th century was Rev. Jesse Mercer.

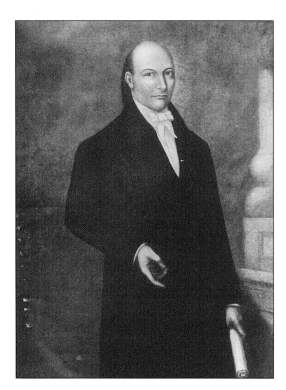

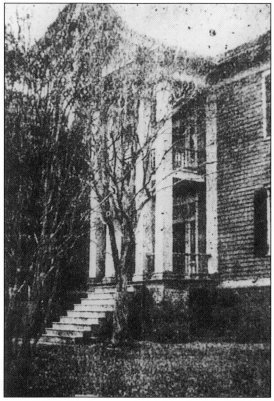

Mercer's home on Academy Hill, just west of town, was later owned by Nicholas Wylie, a wealthy Reconstruction entrepreneur. From Wylie's estate the Catholic Diocese purchased the property and incorporated the old Mercer house into the sprawling building's design. This image shows the house during Wylie's ownership.

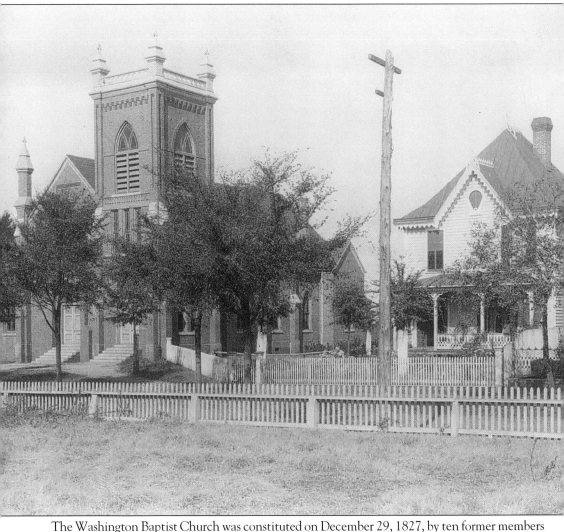

The Washington Baptist Church was constituted on December 29, 1827, by ten former members of Phillips Mill Baptist Church. Rev. Jesse Mercer, one of those instrumental in the church's organization, also served as its first pastor, until his death in 1841. This late 1890s photograph shows the church, built in 1883, and its new pastorium. (Courtesy Mary Willis Library.)

Taken shortly after the Baptist Church was constructed in 1883, this image shows the turrets and finials, which have since been removed during later remodelings. (Courtesy Mary Willis Library.)

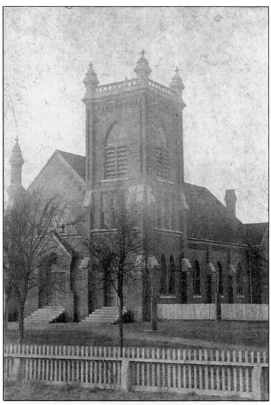

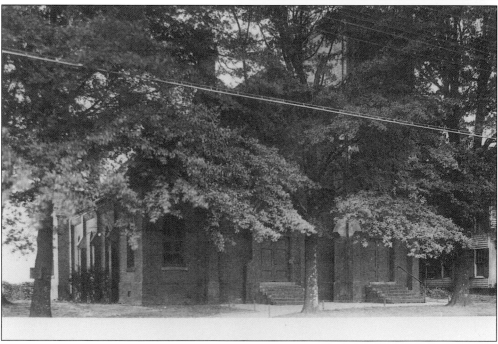

This picturesque 1919 view documents the west side of the building and the shady entrance into the church.

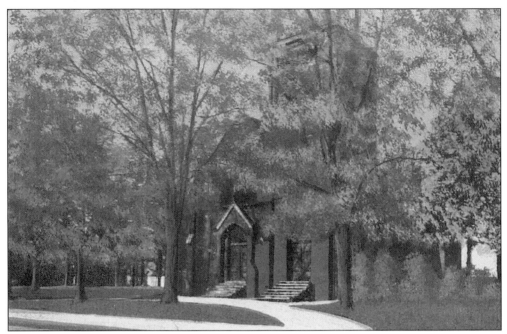

An early-20th-century postcard provides a romanticized look at the Washington Baptist Church. (Courtesy Mary Willis Library.)

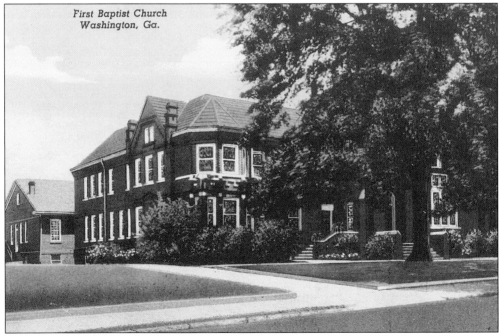

By the 1920s, the Washington Baptist Church had passed the Methodist as the largest congregation in town, and expanded facilities were necessary. This postcard view shows the Grice annex (named after the church's dynamic pastor, Rev. Homer Grice), which altered the west side of the original church. (Courtesy Mercer Harris.)

Seven

LEISURE AND SOCIETY

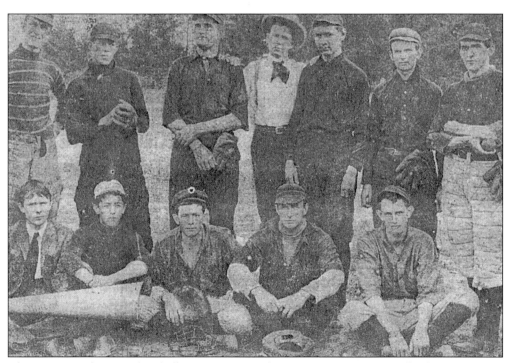

The 1903 Washington baseball team poses with manager Doc Neeson (back row, center, wearing tie). In those horse-and-buggy days when traveling was done at 4 miles per hour, most games were played versus other Wilkes County communities like Rayle, Tignall, and Danburg. Third from the left in the front row is catcher Stoy Jackson, Washington's long-time star.

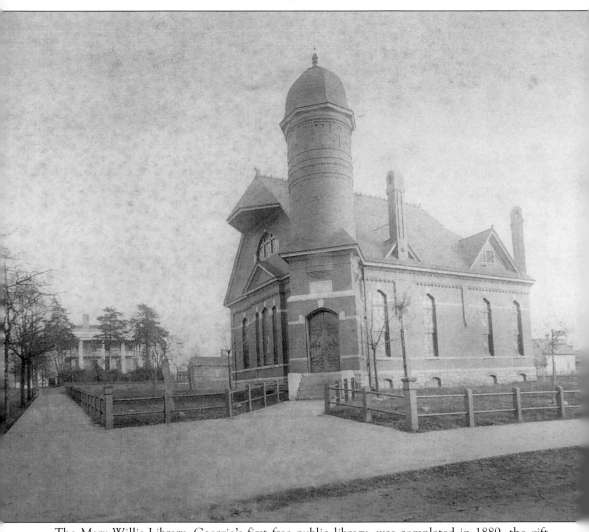

The Mary Willis Library, Georgia's first free public library, was completed in 1889, the gift of Dr. Francis T. Willis to his native city and named in honor of his daughter. The building was designed by architect E.G. Lind. At left in the background is the home then owned by Benjamin F. Jordan. (Courtesy Mary Willis Library.)

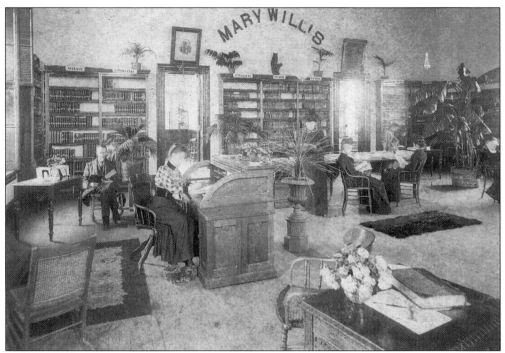

In a picture taken shortly after the library opened, the institution's first librarian, Carrie Dyson, sits at the rolltop desk. At far left is Samuel Barnett. Others in the photograph are, from left to right, Nora Palmer, Mrs. Sarah Cooper Sanders, Mrs. K. Barksdale, Emma Lane, Lucy Smith, Willie Mat Sims, and Eliza A. Bowen. (Courtesy Mary Willis Library.)

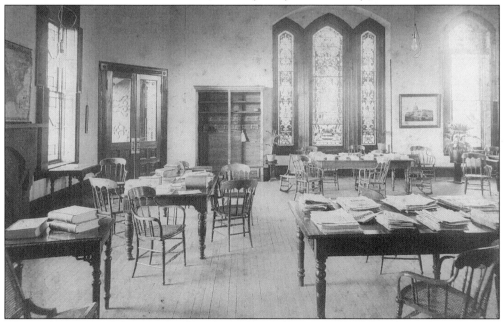

The reading room of the Mary Willis Library featured a spectacular triptych window, executed by the Tiffany Studios, with a center image of Mary Willis flanked by Shakespeare and Homer. (Courtesy Mary Willis Library.)

MARY WILLIS LIBRARY.

ABSTRACT OF RULES.

Books borrowed from the Library may be kept two weeks; and may be renewed unless there are other applicants for them. If not returned when due, a fine of 10 cents per week (or fraction thereof), shall be paid, *unconditionally. The Librarian shall have no discretion on this point.* Excuses may be filed with the Librarian to be acted on by the Trustees, and if satisfactory such fine will be re-funded.

Damage to Books from rough or careless handling shall be assessed and collected by the Librarian. Appeals may be made to the Trustees.

Books of reference shall not be taken from the Library.

Failure to pay fines shall forfeit the use of the Library, and the Librarian shall issue no books to any one in arrears.

Rules were established at the outset for the Mary Willis Library in 1889. For almost 80 years Washington had sporadically supported a library society, but, with the development of this magnificent facility, the Trustees wanted to ensure that it would be operated equitably and efficiently. (Courtesy Mary Willis Library.)

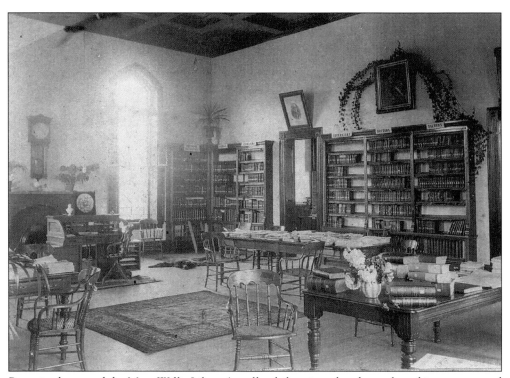

Portraits decorated the Mary Willis Library's walls while oriental and even bearskin rugs covered the floors. It was an inviting and wonderfully Victorian place. (Courtesy Mary Willis Library.)

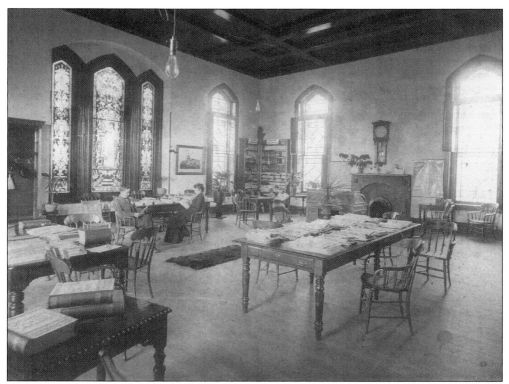
Patrons could enjoy the warmth of the beautifully wrought windows as well as that from the fireplace c. 1890. Note the "modern" inclusion of an electric light bulb dropped from the ceiling. (Courtesy Mary Willis Library.)

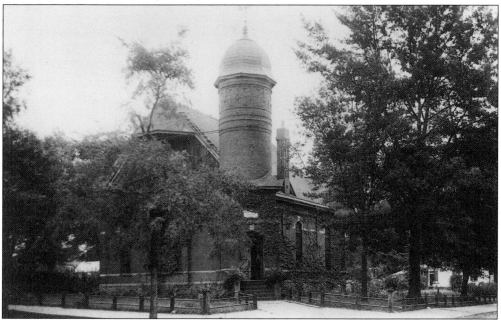
Landscaping around the library was lush in this 1919 view of the distinguished building. (Courtesy Mary Willis Library.)

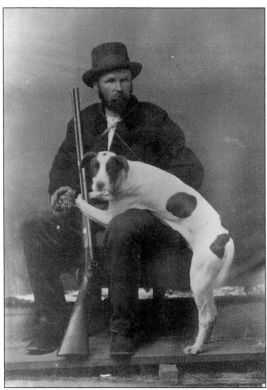

Gideon Norman Strozier sits for a mock-serious portrait with his canine companion and trusty rifle. Strozier entered the Confederate Army as a private in Hill's Wilkes Guards on October 8, 1861. He suffered wounds at both Mine Run and Cold Harbor before surrendering at Appomattox.

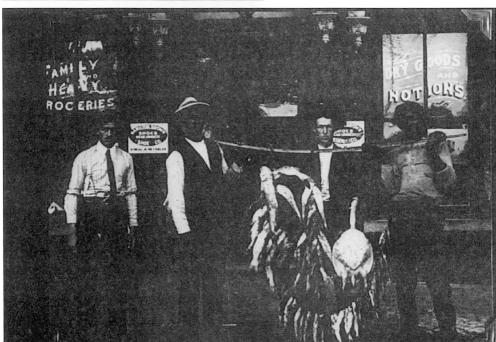

Fishing was not just an activity but a passion for many Wilkes Countians. Here, Joe Maxwell (at left) and Henry Garrett display the fish they caught at Anthony Shoals on Broad River, which separates Wilkes from Elbert County. (Courtesy Mary Willis Library.)

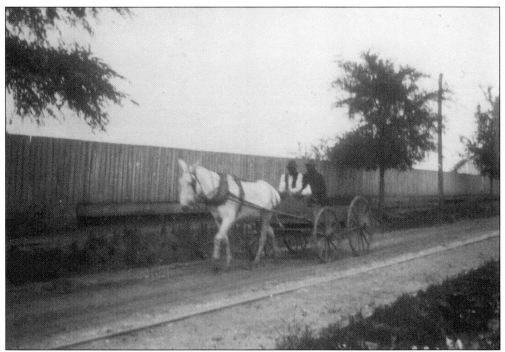

In 1900 the usual mode of travel was mule and wagon. Washington, in fact, had become one of the major mule markets in the South during this era and "goin' to town" was a special treat. (Courtesy Washington Historical Museum.)

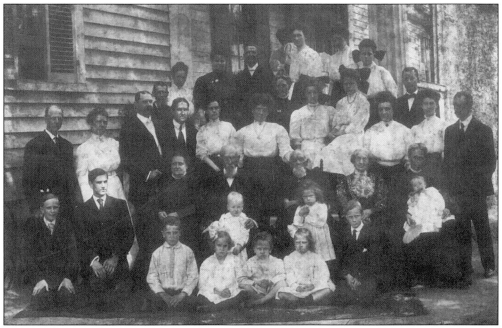

The family of William Wylie Hill gathers for his birthday party in 1907. They are posed on the side porch of "Pleasant Shade," now the residence of Rosalie Haynes on East Robert Toombs Avenue. (Courtesy estate of Mrs. Mary F. Barnett.)

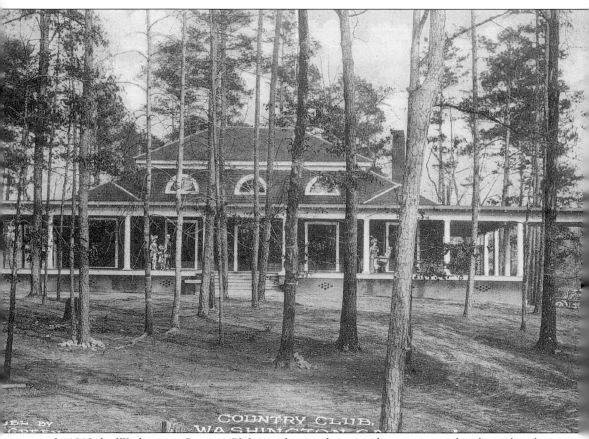

In 1912 the Washington Country Club was chartered to provide a recreational and social outlet for Wilkes Countians. Several locations were examined and a 10-acre tract on Spring Street was selected and purchased for $ 5000. A swimming pool was constructed at the rear. The *Washington Reporter* described the structure as follows: "The club house is of the bungalow type. . . It is attractively furnished and well appointed in every particular being equipped with a large main ball room, two private dining rooms, pool room, shower baths, reading room, and two dressing rooms." Grand opening ceremonies were held on October 28, 1913, with Governor and Mrs. John M. Slaton in attendance. (Courtesy Mary Willis Library.)

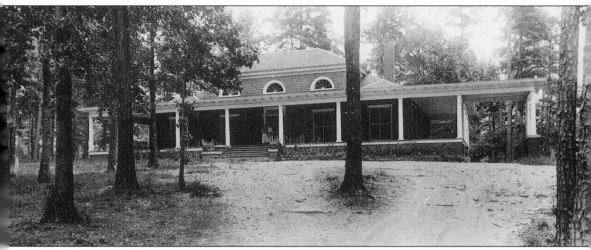

In 1919 the country club porch was an inviting place where many Washingtonians came to socialize.

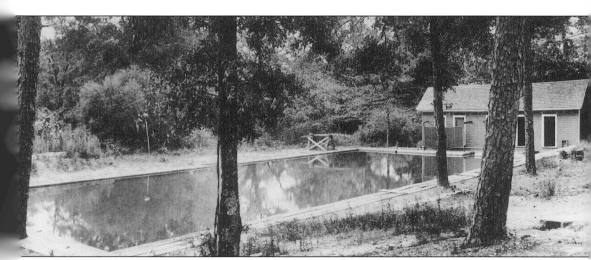

The club's swimming pool and bathhouse were especially alluring to the local young people. A make-shift diving board can be seen on the upper side of the pool.

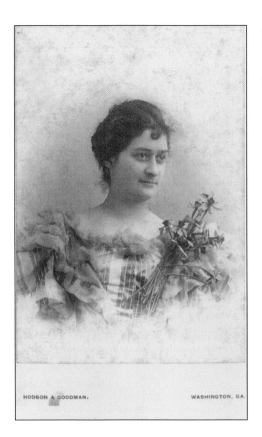

Hodgson and Goodman were popular Washington photographers in the mid-1890s. This young lady wears the highest fashion of the day along with an elaborate corsage.

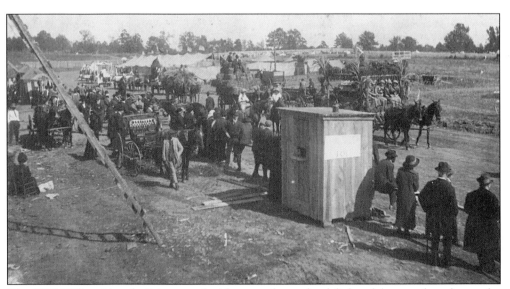

The 1912 Wilkes-Lincoln Fair opened with a parade, to the delight of those gathered near the ticket booth. Leading the procession (at right) is the Washington troop of Campfire Girls. (Courtesy estate of Mrs. Mary F. Barnett.)

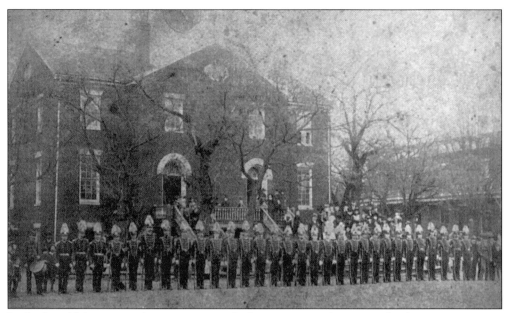

In the late 19th century there was a revival of interest in and support of militia organizations. With great enthusiasm the young men of Washington formed a unit they designated the Irvin Guards to honor their Confederate counterparts. The local troop was then accepted as a part of the Georgia State Militia. In this 1897 view, they stand in review in full military regalia, proudly displaying their new uniforms.

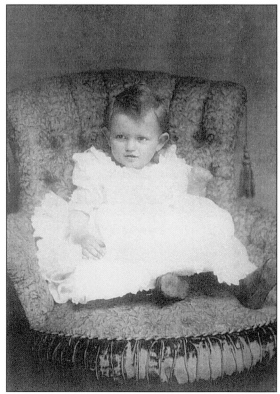

A traveling photographer named Tyzzer came through Washington in the 1890s and provided images for a number of local families. Elegantly outfitted and seated in a Victorian tufted chair, this young boy, a member of the Norman family, poses for the camera. (Courtesy Paula Drexler and Dawn Walker.)

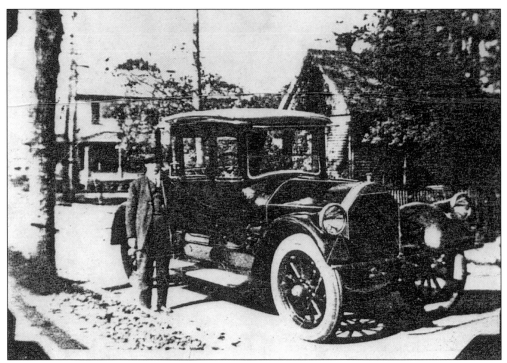

Dr. Robert A. Simpson stands beside his new sedan c. 1920. His residence is out of camera range to the left. In the background at left is the home of Mary Helen Hynes (now occupied by James A. Barnett) and at right is E.Y. Hill's rental house (now occupied by Robert M. Willingham Jr.). (Courtesy Mary Willis Library.)

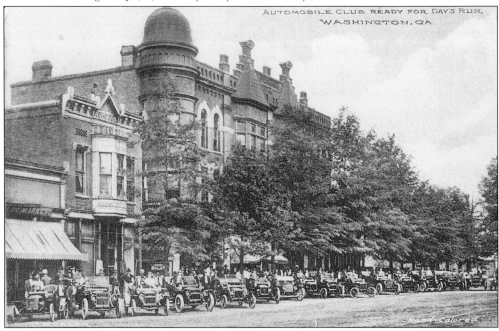

The Washington Automobile Club lines up before the Fitzpatrick Hotel about 1911. A day of touring was a delightful diversion during that era. (Courtesy Mercer Harris.)

In July 1915 Berta Odum bought out J.W. Stephenson's studio, becoming Washington's first female professional photographer. After a course at the Eastman School in 1917, she returned to advertise her competency in "new moonlight and fireside professional photographs." Although the subject of this portrait is not known, the artistic quality is undeniable. (Courtesy C. Carol Cartledge.)

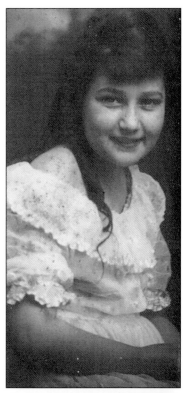

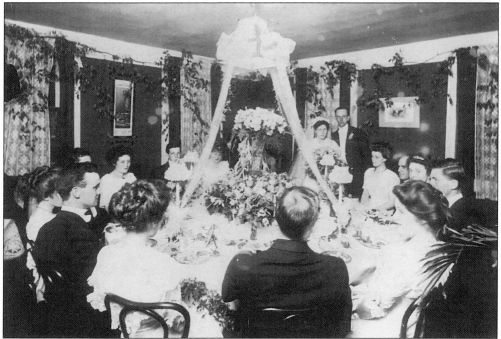

Family and friends came together in sumptuous surroundings to celebrate the marriage of Elizabeth Barnett and Marion Pembroke Pop (standing) on July 7, 1910. (Courtesy estate of Mrs. Mary F. Barnett.)

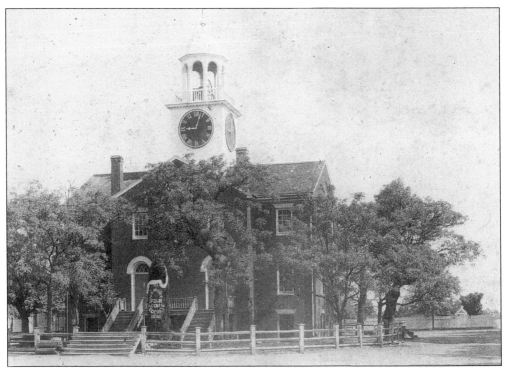

In April 1887, a temporary memorial was decorated to honor the Confederate dead on Memorial Day. The board fence with steps at strategic points (stiles) was placed around the old courthouse to keep grazing animals at a distance. (Courtesy Mary Willis Library.)

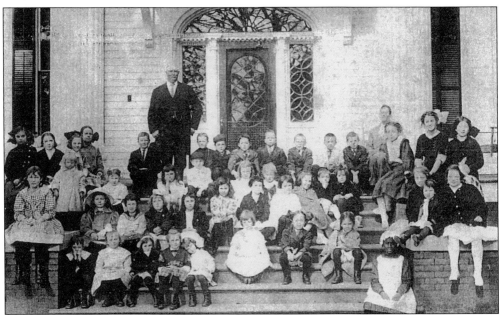

R.D. Callaway (standing on the porch) and Mrs. Callaway hosted a party for the neighborhood children at their new home c. 1911. The home, no longer standing, was one of Washington's most elaborate and elegant. (Courtesy Mary Willis Library.)

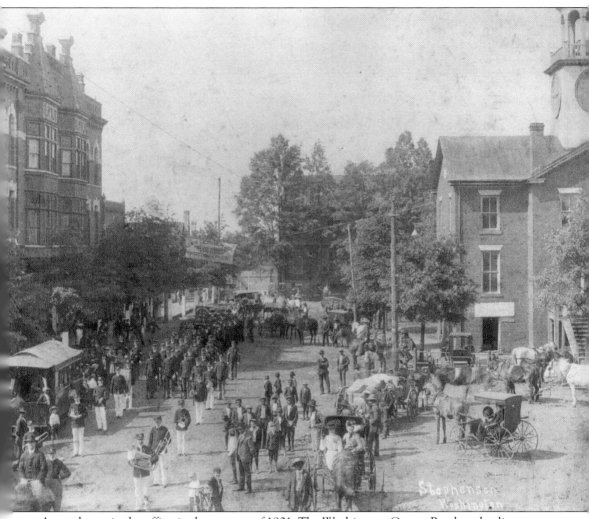

A parade was in the offing in the summer of 1901. The Washington Cornet Band, under director J.B. Laramore, was resplendent in their new uniforms of maroon jackets and white duck trousers. Behind them, the high school boys of the Lee Light Guards precede the old soldiers of the John T. Wingfield Camp of the United Confederate Veterans. (Courtesy Mary Willis Library.)

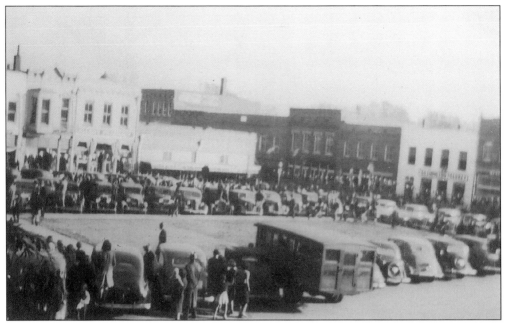

A few decades later, another parade on the square drew a crowd as every parking space was filled. (Courtesy Mary Willis Library.)

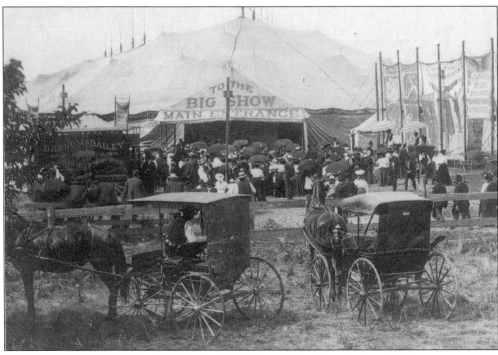

Over the years circuses have brought delight to countless Wilkes Countians. From P.T. Barnum's "Menagerie" in the 1870s to the "big top" extravaganza of Barnum and Bailey (pictured here set up on West Liberty Street near Dublin in the late 1890s), Washington hosted shows that arrived via train on their way to or from wintering in Florida. (Courtesy Mary Willis Library.)

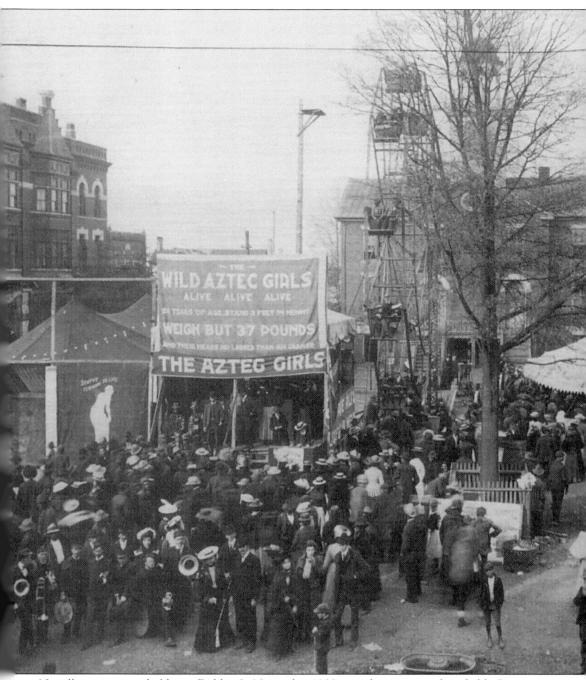

Not all circuses were held near Dublin. In November 1900, an eclectic carnival, probably Cooper and Company's "Monster Railroad Show," established itself on the square and the crowds filled the open space. More popular than even the Ferris wheel were the "Wild Aztec Girls" and the "Statue turning to life." In the foreground is the Washington Cornet Band, which frequently entertained at local events. (Courtesy Mary Willis Library.)

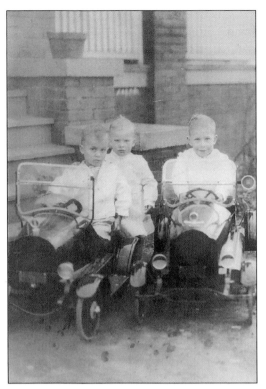

Chase, Charles, and Barrington Ward (pictured from left to right) prepare their own version of the Indianapolis 500 in the early 1920s as they sit behind the wheels of their "child-size" Model Ts. (Courtesy Mrs. John H. Ivey.)

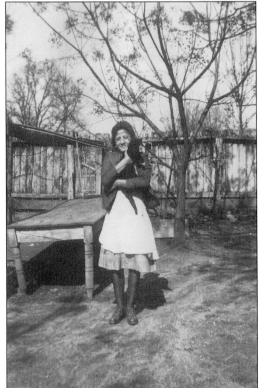

Sallie Handspike holds "Boots" the cat in this photograph taken about 1940. Note the old tavern table at the left, used then for laying out sumptuous picnics and barbecues.

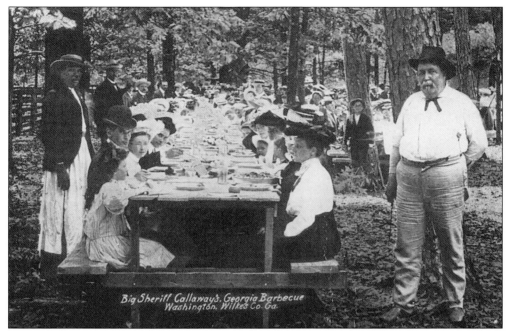

One of the great traditions of Washington-Wilkes for much of its history has been the barbecue with Brunswick stew and all the trimmings. Considered the premier chef of the "true Georgia 'cue" was Wilkes County Sheriff John W. Callaway, a Confederate veteran, who traveled America sharing his culinary expertise. (Courtesy Mercer Harris.)

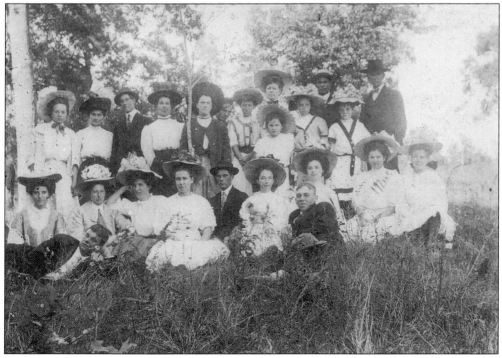

A group of Washingtonians come together for an outing in the countryside. J.W. Stephenson captured this entourage on film about 1910. (Courtesy Mrs. John H. Ivey.)

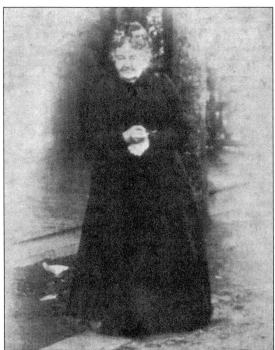

The author of Wilkes County's first history published in 1889, Eliza A. Bowen (1828–1898) was an extraordinarily talented individual who wrote essays for national magazines under the *nom de plume* "Betsy Trotwood" and compiled a widely used astronomy textbook. Although reared in comfortable circumstances, her last years were spent in poverty, dependent upon the kindness of family and friends. (Courtesy Mary Willis Library.)

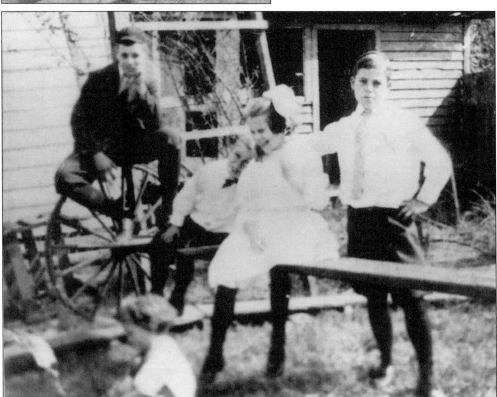

The children of W.T. Johnson enjoy a pleasant time playing outdoors. Pictured from left to right are Hillyer, Buck, Frances, and Rochford Johnson. (Courtesy Mrs. A.D. Duggan.)

"Watching the birdie" about 1916 are Addison Burt (standing) and his brother Clifford. (Courtesy Mrs. John H. Ivey.)

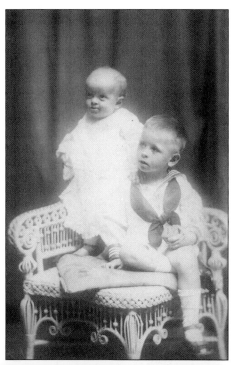

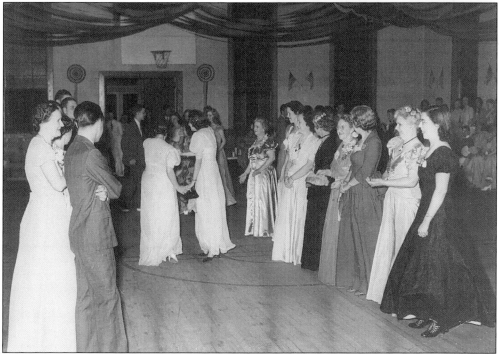

This patriotic dance was held at the auditorium-armory on North Alexander Avenue, probably about 1942. The lady at the left in profile is Mary Helen Hynes, dramatist, teacher, and civic leader, who organized a successful community theater program in the 1930s. (Courtesy Mary Willis Library.)

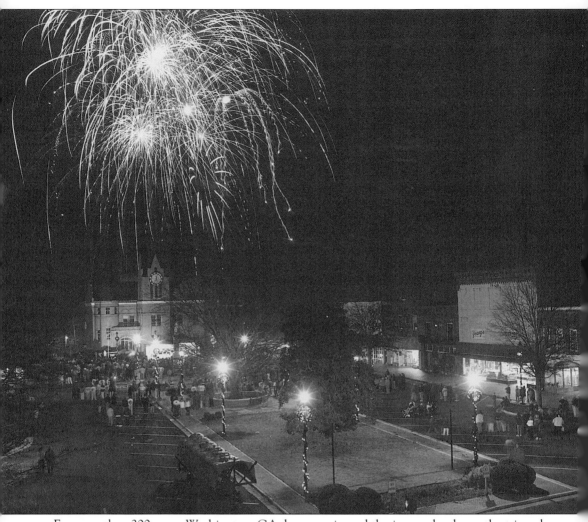

For more than 200 years, Washington, GA, has experienced the joys and sadness, the triumph and misfortune, and the excitement and serenity that all come to make up our history and our heritage. In this Mercer Harris photograph taken at the new millennium, the fireworks over Washington Square symbolize the continued determination of a people united in a celebration of life. (Courtesy Mercer Harris.)